I0264514

William and Jean Herrick
Pioneering New Mexicans

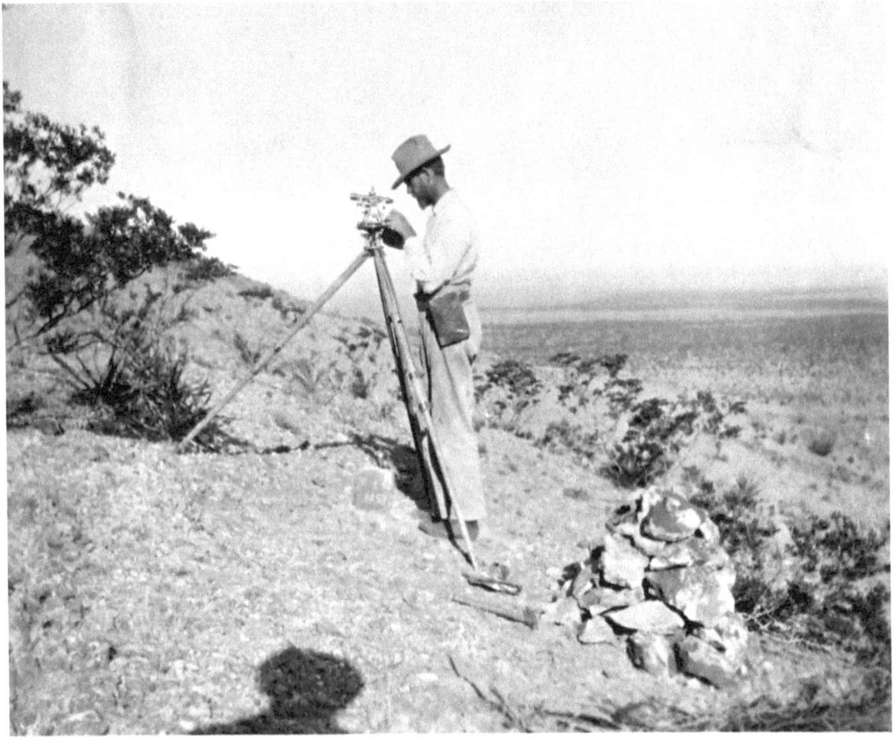

The Herrick Family Words and Photographs
as They Lived and Developed Their Lives
in Early 1900s New Mexico

WILLIAM AND JEAN HERRICK
PIONEERING NEW MEXICANS

THE HERRICK FAMILY WORDS AND PHOTOGRAPHS
AS THEY LIVED AND DEVELOPED THEIR LIVES
IN EARLY 1900S NEW MEXICO

by
MICHAEL SPILLER

SANTA FE

© 2022 by Michael Spiller
All Rights Reserved
No part of this book may be reproduced in any form or by any electronic or mechanical means including information storage and retrieval systems without permission in writing from the publisher, except by a reviewer who may quote brief passages in a review.

Sunstone books may be purchased for educational, business, or sales promotional use. For information please write: Special Markets Department, Sunstone Press, P.O. Box 2321, Santa Fe, New Mexico 87504-2321.
Printed on acid-free paper

Library of Congress Cataloging-in-Publication Data

Names: Spiller, Michael, 1951- author.
Title: William and Jean Herrick, pioneering New Mexicans : the Herrick family words and photographs as they lived and developed their lives in early 1900s New Mexico / by Michael Spiller.
Description: Santa Fe : Sunstone Press, [2022] | Summary: "A family history of William and Jean Herrick, early 20th Century New Mexico Pioneers, who with their family helped shape modern New Mexico"-- Provided by publisher.
Identifiers: LCCN 2022018130 | ISBN 9781632933713 (paperback)
Subjects: LCSH: Herrick, William, 1866-1921--Correspondence. | Herrick, Jean, 1864-1958--Correspondence. | Pioneers--New Mexico--Biography. | Frontier and pioneer life--New Mexico--20th century.
Classification: LCC F596 .S764 2022 | DDC 978.9/040922 [B]--dc23/eng/20220504

LC record available at https://lccn.loc.gov/2022018130

WWW.SUNSTONEPRESS.COM
SUNSTONE PRESS / POST OFFICE BOX 2321 / SANTA FE, NM 87504-2321 /USA
(505) 988-4418 / FAX (505) 988-1025

Contents

1 ~ Introducing the Family
7

2 ~ The Early Years – East of New Mexico
22

3 ~ New Mexico Comes into the Picture
75

4 ~ The Scots Arrive in the New World – New Mexico the First Stop
194

5 ~ The Auto Adds a New Element to Travel
220

6 ~ Will's Death and the Marriage of Two of His Daughters
236

Uncle Clarence's cabin at Hop Canyon, 1903.
Grandma Anna Herrick with Will, Jean, the girls and Mrs. Lovelace.

1
Introducing the Family

Over one hundred years ago to get from Chicago, Illinois, Minneapolis, Minnesota, or Mount Vernon, Ohio, to New Mexico, you had to walk, ride or drive a team of horses or board a train. Time moved at a different pace than today, where one can be on the other side of the world in a matter of hours. Everything took more time. A train trip was an adventure of up to a week of sitting, bumping along with few of the comforts of today's travel. Information traveled only as fast as the fastest horse, the mightiest train and the new age of the telegraph. Photography was also new in the world having been in existence for a short time or so, 1848 was the first photograph. Queen Victoria and the Industrial Age set the manner of the time.

William Howard Herrick (1866–1921) was a true pioneer at the turn of the 20th century, born August 13, 1866 in Minneapolis Minnesota. He was tall and well spoken and the New Mexico Territory was still the Wild West around the 1900s when he arrived. Poncho Via and Geronimo were recent headlines here and across the country. The Galveston hurricane killed eight thousand people. The Wright brothers surprised the world by getting a heavier than air machine into controlled flight. The Panama Canal was built and opened the East and West coasts of America. Europe was on the brink of War. Undertaking the journey at that time was not for the faint of heart. Once in New Mexico, travel was by train, stagecoach, horseback, or by foot through rugged terrain full of mountains, canyons, river crossings and was freezing in the winter and blazing hot in the summer. This was standard duty for a young man of the time, but the families' travels were a different experience. There were few amenities. On the train there was just a hole in the floor in a small room as the bathroom. There were sleeper cars but they were few and expensive. There are few hotels, sometimes none. There were not a lot of comforts to be had while traveling. Buckboards and covered wagons were exactly like their names—drawn by multiple horses and a twenty mile day was a very good day, more like eight to ten miles. You camped along the trail in your blanket roll and tent. They were your motel. You brought everything with you. Your horse was your best friend and had to be well taken care of. Water was your most important resource and your trip must be planned with all that in mind. New Mexico is a high desert and water was and is one of the biggest drawbacks to the population growth then and now.

Will's knowledge and technical expertise in photography is evident in the images he made. It was more than a hobby; it was still a fairly new field and difficult under the best of circumstances. Photography required much training to operate the equipment—understanding the chemistry, as well as money, to afford the equipment and supplies. The images reproduced were passed down to his family. We have continued to photograph life in the Mexico for over 100 years. Glass negatives are fragile and very heavy. The chemicals needed to process the negatives and prints were not readily available. He understood and practiced black-and-white negative and printing processes. Being able to prepare a glass negative with only one half of its surface, ready for exposure, means that he was quite capable. He had the Cyanotype type or blueprint type of photographic printing available, because he was a surveyor. Large size maps and plats are reproduced using the type of process as well as blueprints.

Will, as he was known, came from his an academically talented family. His father was a Union Chaplain in the Fifth Minnesota Regiment during the Civil War and a prominent Free Baptist Minister in an abolitionist church in Minneapolis, Minnesota. His older brother Clarence Luther (C.L. Herrick), born June 22, 1858, was a world renowned naturalist, early environmental scientist, psychobiologic professor and the second president of the University of New Mexico, 1897–1901.

CLARENCE L. HERRICK, M. S.
President and Professor of Psychology and Philosophy

Will's younger brother, Charles Judson (C. Judson) Herrick, born October 6, 1868, was also a renowned scientist and professor emeritus of neurology, at the University of Chicago. With this lineage of academic excellence, Will had a difficult time with Latin and other foreign languages. This is more than likely the biggest stumbling block to his following his brothers into a life in the scientific fields.

C.J. Herrick (Charlie) 1917 or 1918. He is a Major in the Army working at a research hospital.

Will attended Denison University where his brothers were professors at different times and then followed Clarence probably to the University of Chicago. The University of Chicago or Denison University was the most likely place that William would have had the opportunity to learn photography as he did. I have done some research and have not been able to find any other information or possible insight to where William picked up photography, but he did it very well. Somewhere between Chicago, Denison University and Mount Vernon, Will was introduced to Jean Elizabeth Colville (1860–1958). The stories that I heard forever were that Jean tutored Will in Latin and that was the beginning of their relationship. According to my grandmother Sarah Herrick Fraser, her father, Will, while living on the Colville farm designed and built a house for one of the Colville brothers, probably Charles, Jean's closest brother, around 1888, in Mount Vernon. The fall term of 1888 Will's class report card shows he was at Granville Academy which is very close to Mount Vernon so the opportunity would've been very convenient for Will to design and help build this home for one of his to-be brother-in-laws. I do not know which one for they all seem to move around a lot as you will see. He took this photo (below) on a glass negative.

"The house that Thomas Colville was born in. It is in Knox County, Mount Vernon, Ohio. The original cyanotype print (here in black and white) is blue because it was printed on Blueprint paper."

In the fall term of 1881, Will was enrolled at Denison University in Ohio. He used this as a preparatory school studying chemistry, algebra, senior geometry and Rhetoric as classes, and passed by all notations on his report card.

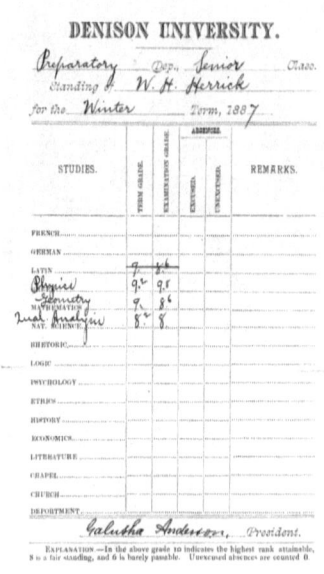

There are also reports of W. H. Herrick attendance and scores for the winter term, 1887, at Denison University. Will then transferred to Granville Academy, also in Ohio, for the term ending December 19, 1888, then he was back it Denison University for the winter term of 1889. He returned to Granville Academy for the term ending June 18, 1889, then returned to Denison University for the fall term of 1893, fall term of 1893, spring term of 1894, winter term of 1894, and his final report for the winter term of 1895 all it Denison University in Ohio.

The letters in my possessions start November 22, 1886.

On November 22, 1886, Carl L. Lachnurd, is updating Mr. Herrick that his new European violin has arrived in the USA and should be in his possession soon.

Minneapolis, Minn. —
Nov. 22 - '86,

Dear Mr. Herrick,

Today I send you the new violin by Express. I regret that you had to wait so long, but the goods were delayed first at Cologne and again two weeks in New York — However they are *very* satisfactory and so we can be *satisfied*. I enjoyed the violins so much, it seemed as though I could not part with them. You will notice the fine regularity of the belly wood and elegant lustre of the back — I marked the bridge and also the sounding post so that if either should fall down you can replace it correctly. The bill of the goods had to be legalized by the Consul at Cologne; on account of this, and some telegraphing I had to do to New York the price comes a little higher than anticipated, but will make it the same to you as promised. The strings are fine too. You will like the untied "Padua" Ex, as also the other italian strings. I make them to you at $1.75 together. $2.00 is what the others are paying, and that is at a reduction.

Let me hear from you

soon so that I will know that the violin has come safely to hand. I have packed it as carefully as possible — Hoping that it may give you much encouragement,

I remain

Sincerely yours teacher

Carl V. Lachmund

N.B.

Prof. Japha of Cologne selected the violin, and said again in his letter that the violins were extraordinary reasonable in price for Germany, and doubly so for America, and praises Staubens excellent workmanship —

In haste.

In spring of 1887 Will and his brothers Clarence and Charlie traveled on a field expedition to the Appalachian Mountains, Gulf of Mexico and Lake Superior taking samples and notes for one of Clarence's studies. This information came from the "Transactions of the American Philosophical Society, New Series-Volume 45, Part 1, 1955."

DENISON UNIVERSITY,
GALUSHA ANDERSON,
PRESIDENT,
GRANVILLE, - - OHIO.

Granville, Ohio, Sep. 20th, 1888.

To the University of Minnesota,

Mr. W. H. Herrick, the bearer of this note, has taken in this University an elective course, of which he will himself inform you, giving you all necessary particulars. He has been faithful and efficient in his work. He is a good man and it gives me great pleasure to commend him to your entire confidence. He is by his own request honorably dismissed from us.

Galusha Anderson,
President Denison University.

William's parents: Henry Nathan Herrick (1832–1886). Henry was born in Morristown, Vermont and Anna Strickler Herrick (1834–1938) was born in Clarence, New York. They married October 1, 1857.

A Daguerreotype of Henry Nathan Herrick, Pre Civil War.

Photographs of the Colville Farm in Mount Vernon, Ohio from glass negative by William Herrick, 1880s or 1890s.

Thomas Colville (1816–1896). Born and died in Knox County, Ohio. Father of Jean (Jennie) Colville Herrick.

Sarah Patrick Colville (1825–1913). Also from Knox County. Married 1847. The mother of Jean and had a sister but I have no other information about her.

2
The Early Years - East of New Mexico

William Luther Herrick, No Date.

Jean (Jennie) Ellen Colville Herrick, 1886.

The following two pages are examples of W. H. Herrick's certificates at the University of Minnesota.

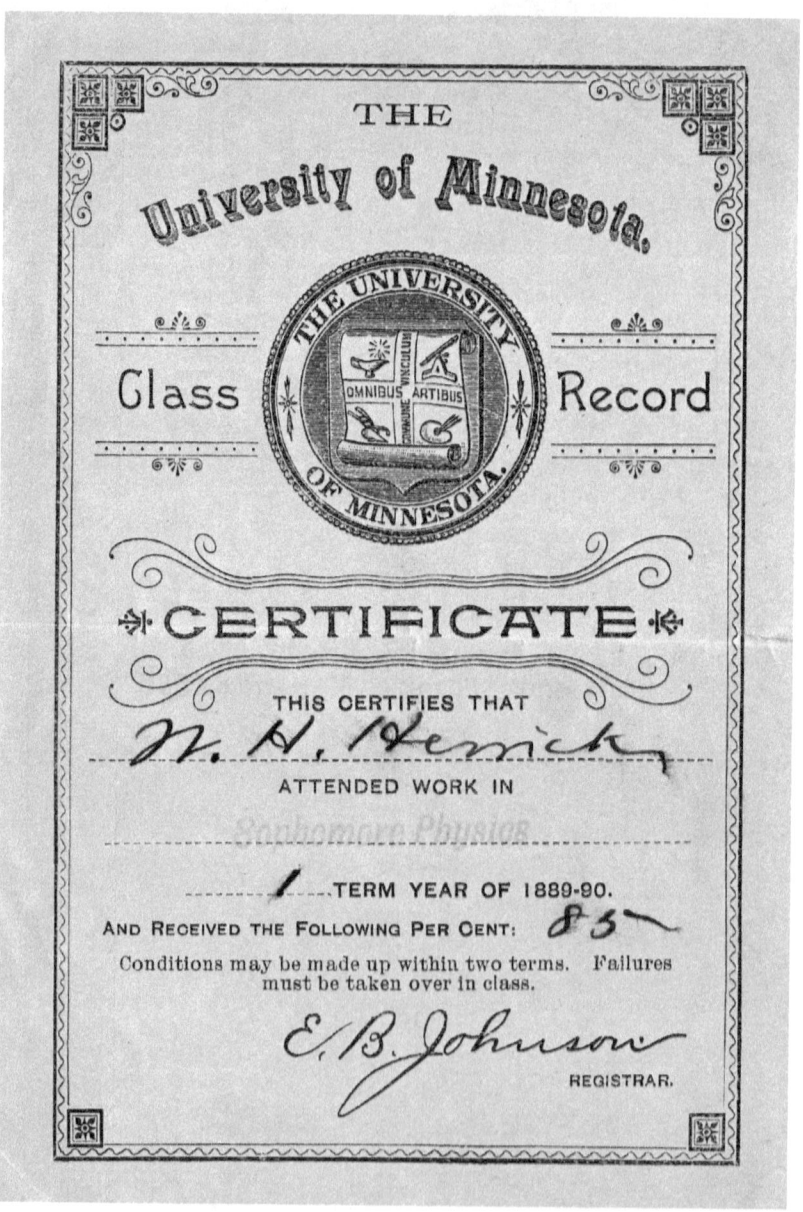

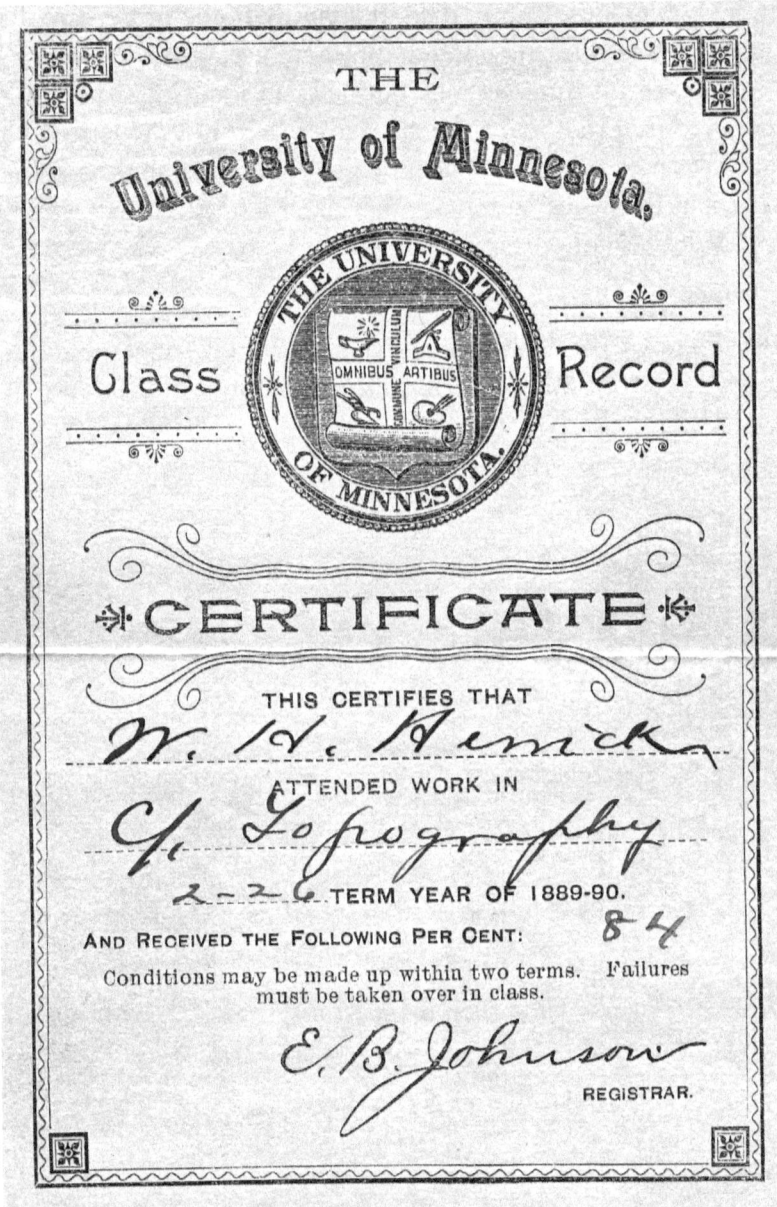

By 1890 William was studying engineering at the University of Minnesota. Jean was about to take on a new job as a librarian at the University of Chicago. Will is shown in the 1890–1891 University of Minnesota catalog and announcement as a student.

When my great aunt, Bunny, died, the family home in Socorro, had to be emptied. I was studying photography and history at the University of New Mexico at this time. Because of this I had some idea of the value of the rooms of stuff that had to be cleaned up. Most of the letters, photos and old negatives came from here, which made this book possible. It's amazing that there was no fire or other natural disaster that would have destroyed all these important documents.

The President of The University of Minnesota on September 4, 1890 acknowledges that Mr. W.H. Herrick was a "Special Student" at the university.

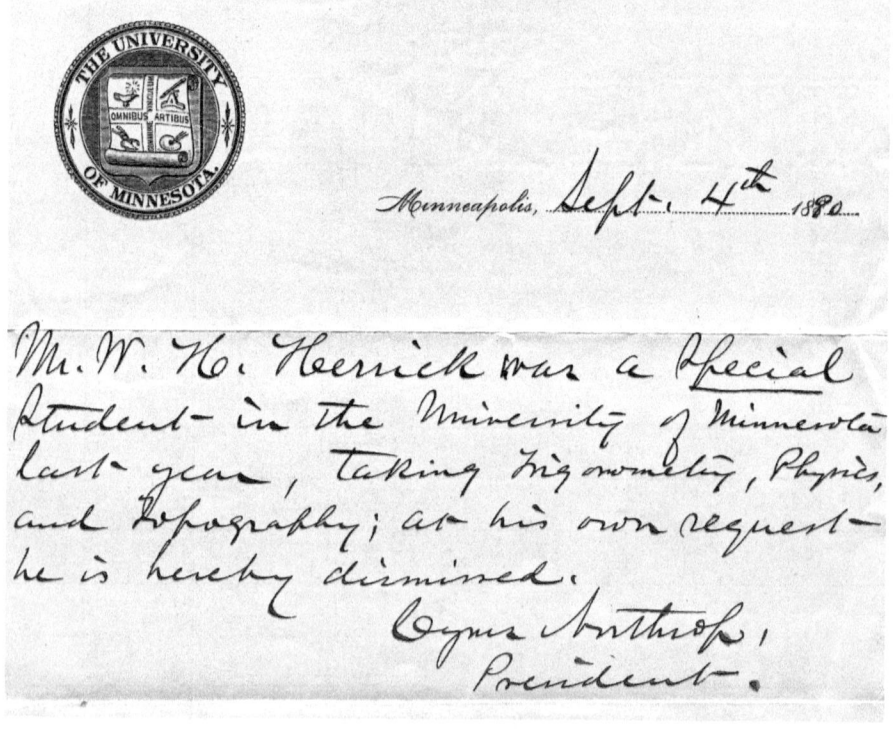

By this time William and Jean are acquainted with each other. These correspondences between them and the photographs that follow will show the amazing history of the family.

This letter is from the Calvary Baptist Church at the corner of 26th Street and Blaisdell Avenue, Minneapolis, Minnesota, September 9, 1890. It certified that the Calvary Baptist Church of Minneapolis Minnesota, by vote at regular meeting August 28, 1890, has granted to Mr. Will Herrick, a member of said church, and its believer to preach the gospel in the many ways open to him. G.L.Morrill, Pastor, Dudlay. Clerk.

From this letter, it is clear that my Great Grandfather is contemplating a life in the clergy much like his father. One of the calling cards I have in my collection is for: W. H. Herrick, Job Carpenter. Storm and screen doors made-to-order 2428 Pleasant Ave., Minneapolis, MN.

W. H. HERRICK

JOB CARPENTER.

—STORM AND SCREEN DOORS MADE TO ORDER.—

2428 Pleasant Ave., - - - - Minneapolis, Minn.

So the idea of his being handy with his hands leads to the next letter that seems to be the most direct comment to him. This is another commonality that I have with my Great Grandfather, I'm a carpenter as well as a photographer.

Ten months later, Will receives a letter from his brother who is concerned over the attitude and life decisions that are in front of his younger brother.

"July 12, 1891

University of Cincinnati
Biology and Geology
C. L. Herrick

Dear Will,

I have felt since leaving Minneapolis that perhaps you might feel that I have shirked responsibility in not advising more specifically that I did in your dilemma. But the truth is that the conditions of the problem are so largely subjective that anyone else might be considerably at a loss how to advise. If you feel it is a duty to preach or enter other distinctively evangelistic work I am unwilling to place the slightest obstacle in your way. If however, you rely like most of us on indications growing out of conscious fitness and environment I should like to call attention to the one or two points which would influence me somewhat.

First. One is most successful in influencing others when he is on ground of conscious superiority and confidence. Do you not think that as a "boss" a superior directing work, you would have a different kind of influence over men there as a professional preacher.

Second. Do you not think that more good can be done in the personal than the public way?

Third. Do you not think that the evangelization of our cities and the mechanical classes must have come from writings? It is a sad fact that mechanics as a classes are practically infidels or agnostics.

Fourth. Do you think that at your time of life you can hope to complete with men who have always had a tendency towards rhetorical and literary pursuits?

Fifth. Is it likely judging from father's experience that your physique will prove adapted to sedentary employment with great nervous strain?

Six. What do you think the effect would be in your circumstances if you should delay five years longer in preparing for practical work?

Seventh. Would you not be following the general path of your preparations thus far if you should enter some profession involving mechanical construction?

Should you not come to Cincinnati this fall it would somewhat this disarrange our plans and prove a disappointment to us here, but I am forced to admit that in view of everything I am not sure that your wisest course is not to continue your engineering studies and to practice as opportunities afford.

Yours truly C. L. Herrick"

Clarence L. Herrick was Will's older brother by eight years and was enough older that by the time Will was acquiring an awareness of world and Will was out of high school, Clarence was already a renowned naturalist and neurologist with many accomplishments and accolades. At the time of this letter, Clarence was a professor at the University of Cincinnati and is concerned about the direction William is about to go in. Clarence had already attended the University of Leipzig, Germany. and was the "Editor" of the *Journal of Comparative Neurology*.

So back to Clarence's letter to Will, July 12, 1891. I say I am grateful that Will took the letter to heart and continued his education, for otherwise I would not be here today to tell this story. This is where Jennie (Jean) Elizabeth Colville comes into the picture. Jean as she is known will become my great-grandmother in history; she was born in June 20, 1864, in Mount Vernon, Ohio. Her father, Thomas and wife Sarah, was a well respected farmer and businessman in Mount Vernon. They had five children, Will, Rob, Charlie, Jean and Jessie and all were well educated due to the family's affluence. Jean would attend the University of Worcester, Ohio, and graduate with a degree in Library Science, on June 23, 1886. Woman with a college education were not common in this day and age.

This is the Commencement Announcement for Jennie (Jean) Colville's college graduation from
The University of Wooster, Class of 1886.

SENIOR CLASS.

COLLEGIANS.

T. S. Anderson,	Kinley McMillan,
E. M. Bowman,	Will H. McSurely,
Chas. E. Bradt,	Clarence G. Miller,
Frank Ward Burgoyne,	F. D. Morris,
J. Franklin Casebeer,	Warren Ramsey,
L. A. Cass,	Walter H. Reynolds,
Jennie E. Colville,	Ellsworth G. Ritchie,
Charles R. Compton,	J. M. Shallenberger,
V. L. Crabbe,	George A. Shives,
John Francis,	Lizzie S. Stevenson,
Sarah E. Geiselman,	Hunter B. Stiles,
Reuben A. Kope,	Hattie Switzer,
Allen Krichbaum,	J. M. C. Warren,
Ulysses S. Grant McClure,	Lizzie B. White,

Leila A. White.

MUSICAL.

Minnie C. Andrews,
Emilie A. Baughman,
L. A. Cass,
Delano Franklin Conrad,
Effie R. Lenington,
Minerva A. Minnich,
Callie Ramsdell,
Nettie Taylor.

The Class of '86's in class photo. At this time my Great Grandmother was known as Jennie on paper, but goes by Jean. She is seated on the ground, third from the left.

Jennie (Jean) Colville in her cap and gown at home.

This is where the two main players in this story must meet. Jean's oldest brother, William Thomas Colville, a professionally trained physician who studied at the University of Leipzig, among other notable universities and this is where the Clarence and William Colville, the two oldest brothers might have met. Clarence for a time also was a professor at Denison University and the contact point between Clarence and Jean's other brothers could have taken place.

To close the circle, Jane receives a letter dated December 11, 1891, from the University of Chicago. In the letter Gella A. Dixon is being welcomed to her new job at the University of Chicago library, which start January, 1892.

W. R. HARPER, President of University.
E. NELSON BLAKE, President of Board.
C. L. HUTCHINSON, Treasurer.
T. W. GOODSPEED, Secretary.

The University of Chicago.

OFFICE: 1212 CHAMBER OF COMMERCE.

Chicago, Dec. 11th 1891.

Dear Jean;

I am sorry to have seemed to have neglected you lately. I assure you it is only seemingly for I have been so busy I have hardly known which way to turn. Miss Jones the third assistant has been sick with pneumonia & Miss Robertson has been taking her place. She is a perfect treasure & I am sure Miss Hall will be delighted with her.

I wish the matter could be decided soon for Miss Robertson has other positions offered & will hardly be willing to wait longer. As I have taken you from them I am anxious they should have a good librarian to take your place.

W. R. HARPER, President of University.
E. NELSON BLAKE, President of Board.
C. L. HUTCHINSON, Treasurer.
T. W. GOODSPEED, Secretary.

The University of Chicago.

OFFICE: 1212 CHAMBER OF COMMERCE.

Chicago,............................189

You will be expected to be in Morgan Park January fifth. I enclose the time-table for the suburban trains. Buy a 25 ride ticket. That makes it cost only 12½ cts. While the single ride costs 40 cts.

Your room is all ready for you. It is at Mrs. L. H. Rogers. on Armida Ave.

Hoping very soon to welcome you to your new work, where I am sure you will be exceedingly happy.

Yours lovingly,

Zella A. Dupon.
Morgan Park,
Ill.

In 1892 the letters are few, July 31. Jean is home in Mount Vernon for the summer; William is at home in Granville with his brother Charles. Will has been reading and studying Latin with Jean tutoring him. In August there is a second letter with no date and Jean is expecting to go back soon to Chicago and work having spent the summer at home. Will asks if he can visit her in Mount Vernon.

Between February and October of 1893 there are over 30 letters between Jean and Will. They are generally letters of getting to know each other and falling in love. Jean is in Chicago and Geneso, Illinois and Mount Vernon, Ohio and Will is in Chicago Illinois, Minneapolis and Howard Lake Minnesota and Granville, Ohio during this time period. I have 167 letters written between the two of them before they are married in less than two years.

Mount Vernon in the spring, from an early glass negative.

April and the start of spring has Will thinking about his and now Jean's future. This letter is the first mention I have found of photography and his "own Brothers being brothers." Clarence now sees Will's problems with foreign languages but his is amazed by his aptitude for photography, which can become a useful tool in Clarence's fieldwork: "value, self-worth, that it could produce an income."

1800 3rd Ave. So.
Minneapolis, Minn April 28'93

Dear Jean:-
I am looking for a letter from you today. It may come in the afternoon mail, perhaps not till tomorrow, but I will not wait I want to write to you.

How is your brother? I hope he is well by this time.

I have not heard from my R.R yet but expect to this afternoon, I am afraid I shall not get the place; but I am thinking quite seriously of going to work on a farm to see how it would seem for a life work. I dread to do it though unless there is a good prospect that we would both like it, for I would feel that I was wasting time if I did not follow that business. Do you think that we could be happy, not have too monotonous a life, have something to keep us out of the dull life that so many farmers endure if we could start with a small farm stocked and all paid for or at least provision made for payment? From my standpoint it seems to me that if we did not have the great load of debt to carry the life on a farm with that diversion of building my own buildings and other mechanical work so neccessiary on a farm would not become too tiresome. I hardly know what to think of it from your point of view. It seems to me that as far as the drudgery of housework is concerned that as soon as it was neccessicary to have hired help on the farm we could have help in the house. I think it could be managed so that you would not have work yourself to death but have some time for outside work Religious work is more encouraging in country places I think. And I

think you could do much good through purely social means, then I should expect that we should have some time, at some seasons of the year at least, for music, reading & perhaps some systematic study.
If it were wise I have no doubt we could engage in, as time would permit without interfering with regular work, some outside work which might be more or less profitable and interesting. Possibly photography, or something that might make life less monotonous.
I am afraid my dear girl would feel quite lonely way out here in the west 800 miles from her home, but she has got pretty well used to being away by this time & it might not be so hard. I feel that I should wish to be out here, because I know something about this country and climate.
You didn't know what a wild schemer I am did you?

I have some project to talk about every time I write. Well I have nothing else to do but think of what I am to do these days, & when I seem hedged up in one way my mind is hurrying about for some other way out, and at the bottom of it all is the great desire to have my dear Jean with me. I am just aching to get hold of you. If I only had you here so I could look into your eyes, and hear you talk to me and pet you and have you look real happy and sweet I should be so happy. Don't you see how I can hardly wait till I can make a place for you? Yet I don't think I am going to let this great haste make me choose a short cut that I shall be sorry for later. Every plan I have thought of seems to mean at least a years' delay

Unless I should get a permanent place on the R. R. and you would be content to live with me on quite a small salary.

Does it begin to seem all right for me to connect you with my plans in this way so much.

We feel that we are going to marry each other before long, do we not? It seems to me, almost as though we were already because I feel that we are united in heart.

Write me just what you think about this farming business for I think if you are to be my wife you should have something to say in the matter & you have had more experience than I too.

If I should get a position on the R.R. today I suppose that might settle it. ~~for the present.~~

As the Spring comes on I think more & more of the freedom of out of doors. The Sun has finally broken

Have found that there is no place for me on the B.R. expect to go tomorrow into the country am very certain about farm work will be back first of the week I think will let you know what happens envelope. Your Will.

through the leaden sky we have
had so long. It is a very welcome
sight, but it reveals lots of mud
The grass is getting green, but
we are much behind the woods
and fields we tramped over nearly
three weeks ago. It seems an age
since then. I am afraid it will
seem longer before the next time
But we shall be happy in our love
if that happiness is not completed
by being able to touch each other
and look into the loved eyes.
I did not send the book I spoke of
because I thought possibly I might
be going back to, or through Chicago
then I should have stopped with you &
perhaps read the part to you which I
liked. Will send it soon now. You
must not read much so read only the
text in the grammatic form, possibly
skim the chapters III & IV. perhaps I can
mark some paragraphs which will give
you the gist of it
                    Your Will.

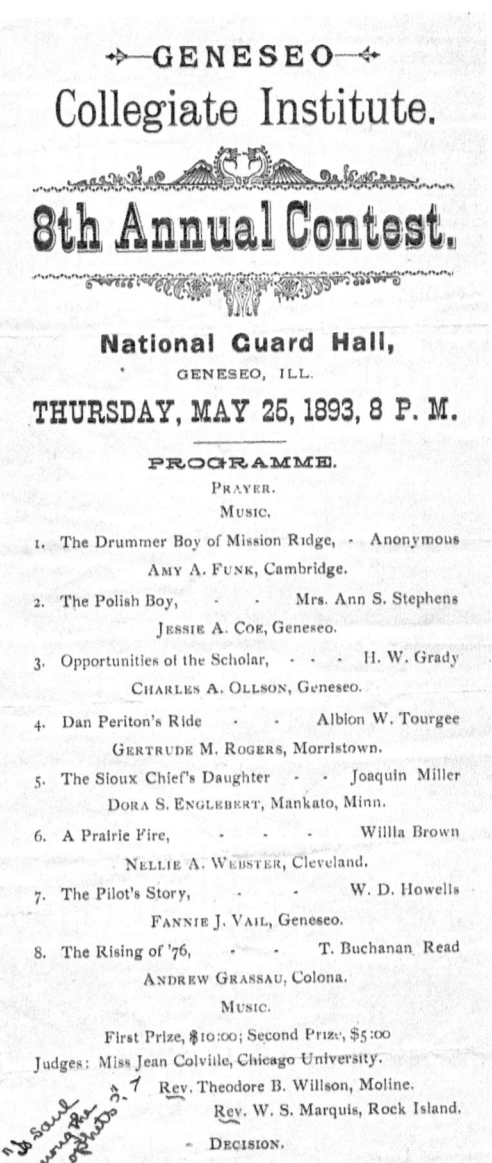

Thursday, May 25, 1893, 8 PM. It seems Miss Jean Colville, Chicago University, is one of the Judges for the "8th Annual Contest" sponsored by the Geneseo Collegiate Institute. It is being held at the National Guard Hall, Geneseo, Illinois, where the "First Prize" is "$10:00" and the "Second Prize" is "$5:00." As you can see by this is flyer that this must be a reading-oratory contest.

By October of 1893, William is a Sales Representative for the Bureau of Laboratory and Natural History Supplies; it is part of the Bureau of Laboratory and Natural History Supplies under the supervision of the Scientist Department of Denison University. Will must have had help from his brothers and their reputation getting this job, but as with many of his endeavors, it was not as a lifelong occupation. He was living with his brother Charlie in Granville, Ohio at this time as well. He is enrolled in Denison for the fall term. His letters state that these working very hard at his job and at school.

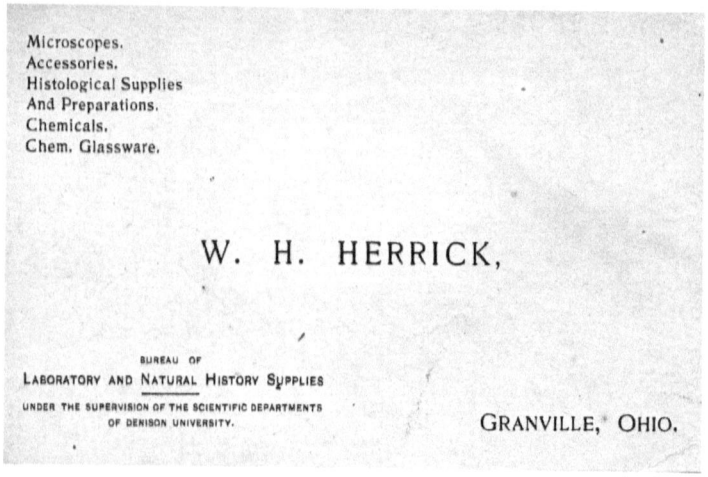

During October of this year, Jean writes about the World's Fair that's in Chicago, and complaints about the crowds: "I took one hour and 20 minutes, each night crowds are awful," to get home from the University library.

November 1893, Jean writes that her sister, Jessie Star's husband, Newt, had passed away and that she was going to Mount Vernon to be with her sister.

December 8, 1893, Will is Granville and writes to Jean in Mount Vernon about a beautiful plaything Clarence received named "Ludwig's Kymograph" that will cost the University $200. It consists of a cylinder which is kept in uniform revolutions by a clock. It is intended to receive the records of many physiological and psychological experiments.

There is a letter on 10 December to Jean's oldest brother:

> "Dear William, we were glad to get your last letter though rather blue it makes me think you are in some ways very much like myself but some ways very much unlike me I am always very cheery, mother and I are very well. We rise at four o'clock in the morning and at 4:30 we have a cheerful fire and at five we have humble, wholesome breakfast after which we take down some good old Bible—reading a portion—then humbly bow before our heavenly father in prayer, always remembering you and all your children in our prayers-then we are ready for the labors of the day, and go on our way always rejoicing and yet I am of ten in tears. I do not think you ought to be discouraged by the tears-bring "too full for utterance." The man that sheds no tears has no heart. I am frequently obliged in reading the Bible to pause in my reading to regain control of my voice especially in reading the latter part of this seventh chapter of Luke. Perhaps when you break down in your class you have more power over it then you ever had before. Don't give up, you don't know what an earnest purpose may accomplish with the word of God in your hands. I once taught a class of six girls and I don't know whether a single word I ever said to them had any impression, but they are now all in the church-all married all mothers training children of their own-training them up I trust in the "nurture and administration of the Lord. We have been having quite a little winter—a week sleying yesterday was warmer.
>
> "Charles and Docie were out this p.m. Charles had letter from Jean. She said she is all right and things are moving along smoothly but they have more work than they can do. You ask several questions about her which I will answer as far as I can in the order asked. I don't know when she will be married he wants it next fall. He is a kind of mechanical genius-make some mathematical instruments. His brother is a great anthropologist and he works for him, and

they furnish books for the college at Granville. He began going to school there intending to a preacher - got partly through his studies- couldn't bear the confinement and was sent out to preach-worked too hard and broke down through nervous exhaustion and had to quit. Is studying now however with view of taking a degree. He will travel around the summer for his brother collecting specimens for his treatise on anthropology. He is talking about building a house at Granville-is a carpenter himself and work some on it himself. I didn't like him very much the first time he was here but every time he comes I like him better than I did before and I believe he is a good, earnest and wholesome fellow and thinks everything of Jean and is just about her age. He was born in Minneapolis Minnesota and is the son of a Baptist preacher-was raised on a farm and worked at the Carpenters business some. I have seen his brother who is a professor at Denison University and is a very good-looking man. This is all I know about William H Herrick. Much love to Lillian and Kenneth from Mother and Dad "

The last letter is the only letter I have from Jean's parents or any other member of her family and it is wonderful for their perspective of their future son-in-law.

December 16, Christmas is coming; Jean is still at 4101 Grand Blvd., Chicago.

"Dearest: Shall I come home for Xmas? "Das ist die Frage." Can we wait to see each other until February or shall I come next Friday night Cora does not take her vacation now because she says she can't afford to go home. I can get away if I want to do so. I thought I would have a letter from my dear boy last night telling me he was well again but it did not come. I trust that this does not mean any harm, I do not think it does. I shall have one tonight anyway. With much love, Jean"

December 23, Will is in Granville and Jean is in Chicago still. Clarence is very ill; he has been hemorrhaging and his lungs are in poor condition. Dr. Charles and Will are keeping the severity of his condition from Alice as her confinement is near.

December 24, Jean is unhappily in Chicago and Will is preparing for Christmas in Granville. She is disappointed and lonely at the fact that they will not be together for Christmas. People are sick in every household.

Christmas, December 25, 1893, Jean starts her letter:

> "Dear, dear boy: I have just received your Friday and Saturday letters. I am so sorry you were so frightened about me and nothing in the world wrong with me-however as I said this I think about that way of putting it, that you would prefer the scare without cause than with it. I'm so sorry don't worry over Clarence. What a sad Xmas for Alice! But I hope you are right that he is not in danger and he will be better soon. I am having such a happy Xmas already yet I hate to say it when I'm thinking how anxious and worried my love must be. I'm waiting for Cora now and Mrs. D. has gone to the Arnold's. I do not expect the mail and to have it come fill my cup with happiness. I'm sorry for the poor postman who has such a hard day he said he has to come again and will bring some packages for me if I am to be home so I am wondering what else. Belle Bevier sent me "Stories from Italy." Did you not say something to think about that little book last year or was it something else. I didn't see why Cora does not come it is 11:30 I hope her arm is not worse with it vaccination. I do hope I will hear good news from my boys dear one soon.
>
> "Our suite happy day is over and I enjoyed it I know and I feel we satisfied Cora did to. Our dinner was good too-if I did not get it myself and there I have received for pretty woman work things over the table this Christmas, they are so pretty I am delighted. You should see the table with ornaments when you come to see

me. You may be sure my heart and thoughts have been with you lover today. May God keep you and yours Dearest. Good night J."

December 27, Granville:

"Dear Jean, I'm expecting a letter from you sweet girl this afternoon but I think you will be anxious I will write now before I go for your letter.

"Our sick one is better, he has had no bleeding for 56 hours and the symptoms indicate that the healing process has begun. We feel much relieved but not very confident. Though I think really that the danger is passed. Xmas day was a very anxious one for the hemorrhage was the worst he had had, and to make matters worse the doctor, without any facts at all, frightened Alice very much so that I had six people to look after instead of one but she felt better the next day. I think most of her worry now, is how to get through her coming sickness and not let Clarence know and worry about it till it is all over. That will, in a few days now I suppose through naturally I don't know much about that affair.

"Last night for the first time since last Thursday I slept for six continuous hours. I was not used up or sick for I had been sleeping for 4 to 6 hours every night though they were dilatched but Tuesday night I found myself not quite so reliable about walking I would wake from 10 to 30 min. late so I asked Charles to come up and sit till 12 o'clock I slept soundly till that time but woke just one minute before 12 and though Charles and called me but he had not for the rest of the night my alarm worked to the minute so I consider that my sleep was made up. I think however that Charles will sit up a while tonight so I can get some continuous sleep. I must keep all right as I am afraid we will have to keep this up for some time. Yes love I'm like your time for coming home all be powerfully good to see you and hold you in my arms. Won't it be jolly!!! You must come about the last of January on Saturday then I will see you over Sunday.

"Then go to see Beulah and be back home than next Saturday and then stay your second week at home and I will see you that Saturday and Sunday if you dare stay over Sunday. That will give us the time to be happy together. Do these sweet meetings make my love more lonesome between whiles? I don't believe they do me. Darling they do me much good. You left your boy very will well when you went back to Chicago and nice stays well this whole month and expects to all next month. You are the best of medicines for a lovesick boy. It is sweet and very pleasant medicine to take too. I must not write more for I must go over to the University to work. I must do some work to keep my strength up. I love you Jean and are very happy in it. Will"

Interior photograph of the Mount Vernon home with unknown young men but could be younger brothers and or friends.

Will opens his December 31 letter with "This is the last letter I will write you this year. Next year at this time I hope we will not be so far apart and will not need to write to each other."

Granville, Dec 31, 1893

My darling Jean:—

This is the last letter I will write you this year. Next year at this time I hope we will not be so far apart and will not need to write to each other. Today is one of those times when I would enjoy most of all simply to have my arms about you and feel your cheek against mine and say nothing. I have nothing to say. If you were in my arms I would tell you much and yet not speak.

Don't worry about me thinking I am blue today for I am not. I am simply tired and inert. Perhaps I should sleep but don't feel much like it.

I wonder what my love is doing

now. Maybe she is writing to her lover now at two o'clock. I wonder if she is or is taking a nap like a good baby. Maybe she has company or Mrs D. is talking to her. Well I hope she is happy. Such a good sweet girl! I like to think about you Jean. I would like to hold you and not have to think about you better. I am afraid if I keep on in this way my letter will sound a little spoony, ain't you? Clarence is still getting better He is getting stronger though of course there is still great danger of taking cold or of his overdoing which might have serious results. Nothing else has transpired in the house yet.

Friday Charles and Mary were in Columbus to see Mother. They found her feeling very well. Perhaps better than usual. Mary said she showed her now. Maybe she is writing to her love now at two o'clock. I wonder if she is. or is taking a nap like a good baby. Maybe she has company or Mrs D. is talking to her. Well I hope she is happy. Such a good sweet girl! I like to think about you Jean. I would like to hold you and not have to think about you better. I am afraid if I keep on in this way my letter will sound a *little* spoony, ain't you? Clarence is still getting better He is getting stronger though of course there is still great danger of taking cold or of his over doing which might have serious results. Nothing else has transpired in the house yet.

Friday Charles and Mary were in Columbus to see Mother. They found her feeling very well. perhaps better than usual. Mary said she showed her

Drummond with great satisfaction
I sent a note by Chas. telling
her about the book and handkerchief
and answering some questions
about you and your family
which she had asked in a previous
letter. By the way have you told
your folks about mother yet? If
you have not perhaps I better
try to tell them when I am there
next if an opportunity offers.
Not a very pleasant thing for
either one of us to do but perhaps
it would come most naturally
from me.
I have been lying on the bed
reading "Tale of Two Cities" this
morning. I have not got very
far but while the story seems
very familiar from a previous
reading yet the details and

style is very interesting. I have done no reading this vacation nor any of the work I had planned. I don't seem to have any energy now that I have time during the day Perhaps I have used up a great deal of energy in watching and carrying the responsibility. Now that Clarence is better I don't have the same anxiety or care I throw it all off during the day and only take it at night. Darling I love you very much I know you love me and I am happy.

Yours Will.

1894 was a landmark year for Will and Jean. Their blooming romance is still a little bit of a long-distance romance but it seems to be growing with every letter.

The January 25 letter starts:

> "My Dear Will, your letter came this p.m. as I worked around here at odds and ends and pack my trunk. Still have neuralgia but if I can only get to Ohio and then West Virginia seems to me the pain must all leave under such warmth as I am sure I must find. Have vacation today after 11 AM Day of Prayer. I had intended to stay some service but included it would be better for me to stay in. We go to the YM and Dwight W tonight and then tomorrow night!! Want a thankful child I'll be there when I am once on the train for home. Only one night after this till I shall see my beloved boy. Yes dear I would like to see your mother but do not know if practical. We will talk of it when we meet, everything turns to the time now I have much to do before time to go to the meeting and must stop. God bless you my own dear boy. Jean"

There are various letters between the two of them in January and February. Jean travels to West Virginia to visit her lifelong friend Beulah Boyd Richie in the end of January. Work does not let Jean stay away for more than a few days. During this period, Clarence is still ill; consumption or TB is hard on him.

March 4, Jean's letter starts:

> "Oh Will my darling boy I am simply longing and restless for you. It seems as if I can't do anything but keep my mind on anything. I even wish it were Monday so I could work than I could keep from longing for you but when it is simply a question of doing what I choose and not bring dinner I just think of and long for you. If I had been told a year ago that I would ever love you like this I could not have believed it. That when I was to think I would simply look upon all time through which I must be separated from you as so much time to be endured until I can be with you again? I think when it's such is the case it is time for us to be married

there is no use in putting it off longer for it must come where people live for each other like that and when separation seems to take away part of our lives, the sooner they are married the better. Alas is only half a life and half its usefulness must be impaired under such conditions. You may never say these words but they expressed some of the intensity of my feelings, possibly writing may relieve the pressure of strong feelings which perhaps only gather strengths from being held in check that's not out allowed expressions because the more absorbing.

"The nature shut up within itself with not another soul near it in which to confide because too full for its own good—even though it is one which does not demand so much sympathy as many others, as the average perhaps."

This letter is unsigned. Jean is in Chicago at this time.

On March 5, Will's response from Granville:

"Dear Jean: my darling girl writes about so many things that I am so anxious to reply to and I have so little time to do it in, or rather no time for I should be studying but I must say some of the things they want to while I am so much in the mood. First, about visiting you, I don't see how I can get away but on account of exams but I may get away before Wednesday, I cannot tell till the schedule for exams is posted. We may get a little time together if she is there. I think if it is impossible for me to get there before she does I better not go be for Wednesday evening for I have so much to do.

"My beloved, I have been thinking about going to Minnesota to build a house, I received no information yet and a letter from Uncle Albert today makes me think I cannot tell whether it will be best till spring really comes. But there is not the slightest doubt but that would be the very best thing for my health, so if it proves practical from a financial standpoint I think I am bound to do it. Now darling how will that affect our plans. In the first place I certainly would not come from 100 miles North of Minneapolis clear to Ohio be married and go back again. We would have to give up our Western trip for this time. In the next place I ought to go just as soon as I can get away in the spring. I am afraid I cannot possibly get away before the first week in June. That would give very short summer to build a house. Even if Clarence is there and has the foundation already and the lumber on the ground I am afraid I could not leave the middle of August until September 1 but if you could only come to St. Paul and be married there in the middle of August that would give us our trip and we could come home by way of the lake September 1. In the meantime I did see the finishing of the house. Or still better if we could be married June 1 and go together to Minneapolis and keep house for the summer, with that be jolly. The most trying thing about this is that we can't know till May probably. We have to "wait for something to turn up "I am not planning much on this game but want to be ready for it if it should be wise. I think we will have too this regard it pretty much in our plans, though it well to have it in mind. We can discuss it better when we see your loved eyes and kiss those lips.

"I want to say something about what to do with your goods but don't feel sure and want to think of it more carefully, besides I should be at work, good night darling my love even if all the wise men in the world say no I am sure I would be better with my girl I have feelings for her. I think too if we take proper air, exercise etc. I will be all right. I have worried you. The case is not hopeless in fact there is no good reason why I should be sick if we had the right kind of life.

Yours Will"

Jean's March 8 letter, starts as many of her letters do with Will "my dear boy am so weary and my head aches so I wish I could lay it on your shoulder but I can't so there is no use wishing." And again in her March 10 letter in the header sideways it states "if you love me take care of yourself in every way, as I know you will and do not let the blues make you act rationally. May God keep you." Jean is working hard at the library.

The letters between the two of them in April continue to discuss the realities of marriage. Classes are keeping Will busy. They continue to discuss wedding plans and toward the end of the month Will writes that Clarence is down again and also has malaria and taking large doses of quinine.

As the letters continue in May, Jean is still in Chicago and Will is in Granville. The wedding is down to being June 14 or June 15. May 27 in a letter from Will to Jean, the date is set for June 15. In Jean's letter to Will on the 28th of May, Jean has her wedding dress.

Jean and friend in front yard of someone in Mounr Vernon, Ohio, ca. 1880-90's

As the wedding day gets closer, Jean is preparing to leave the library in her letter to Will, dated June 2.

Then on June 15, 1894, William H. and Jean Colville are married in Mount Vernon, Ohio.

William Howard Herrick,

Jean Elizabeth Colville,

Married

Friday, June fifteenth,

eighteen hundred and ninety four,

Mt. Vernon, Ohio.

At Home

after July fifteenth,

Granville, Ohio.

On July 29, 1894, Will's brother Clarence, Alice, his wife and son Henry arrived in New Mexico with hopes of recovering from consumption or TB. The dry air and warmer temperatures are said to be advantageous in the recovery of tuberculosis, so the older Herrick's family moves to Socorro, New Mexico.

Will and Jean take up residence in Granville. Mid-August Jean is in Mount Vernon visiting her family before they leave on a trip. I have no information about the newlyweds or any honeymoon, hoping that they had fun for the affection that they showed each other in the letters leading up to this.

Will continues with school for the winter term of 1895, enrolled at Denison University. He has a letter from Clarence confirming that he is in Socorro and Will is trying to advance in school.

> Socorro, New Mexico.
> Jan 24 1895.
>
> This is to certify that Wm H. Herrick successfully completed the work in ~~Freshman~~ Sophomore Zoology at the University of Cincinnati and also a second term with the Juniors and Seniors besides some work in instrument construction in physiology and neurology.
>
> His work might be fairly regarded as an equivalent of two terms in cognate lines in Denison University as now offered.
>
> C. L. Herrick
> Late Prof. Geol. & Biol. Univ. Cin.

As the photographs show, Will and Jean are together for a time at the University of Chicago Library. The double expose pictures of Jean serving tea to herself and other images must've been taken after they were married. It probably wasn't appropriate to make this type of photograph of him and an unmarried woman before they were married.

First side note: Hugh Chapman Frazer is born in Inverness, Scotland April 1, 1895; this amazing man was my grandfather.

June 1, 1895, Beulah Colville Herrick is born in Mount Vernon, Ohio. The next wondrous generation of Herrick's has entered the world.

Clarence opens an office in Socorro for consulting geology and mineral surveying in August of 1896. He also becomes a professor at the New Mexico School of Mining and Technology, teaching classes. His health seems to be doing better. This office will become the Security Title & Abstract Company.

The two of my great grandmother Jean are just sitting enjoying each other's company.

Here Jean answers the door for herself in the first of these double-exposure photos.

Will's photographic technique is totally at work here, where he has to emulsify one half of the glass negative, stage and make the photo, then develop the negative. Once that is done you start over again.

The tea party continues with the dividing line a little more noticeable.

This is an early photo of
The New Mexico School of Mining & Technology, 1890 or 1900s

On July 1, 1897, Clarence L. Herrick becomes the second President of the University of New Mexico in Albuquerque, New Mexico.

The New Mexico's Territorial Governor Otero instructs President Herrick to start the first geological survey of White Sands in the Tularosa basin; this is more work for William in New Mexico.

This photo is from a glass negative that was a bit over exposed of a wagon and horse in front of a rock bluff. Clarence used Will's photographic abilities to add to the report on the Tularosa Basin and White Sands.

Col. State Hospital,
September, 12, 1898.

My Dear Folks,

I write to save you needless ~~trouble and expense with the shawl I left~~, for I fear you will not heed me in regard to what I said concerning the things I left. I did intend to take the shawl but it was mislaid and forgotten. I do not need it and do not want it sent. I once had a garment sent to me when the expressage cost more than the garment was worth. I have two small shawls and a good cloak. My folks here say they are glad to have me come back and I am content. Do not worry over me. God be with you till we meet again. Do not put Him away. Affectionately,

Anna Herrick.

This interesting letter from Will's mother dated the 12th of September, mentions that she is about to be released from the Col. State Hospital.

On October 26, 1898, my most favorite great-aunt Marjorie Herrick Bradbury is born in Mount Vernon, Ohio. She was quite an amazing lady. She married a mining engineer from New Mexico's School of Mines where she grew up in Socorro. She also lived throughout South America.

The 1900 United States Census shows William living in Pleasant, Knox, Ohio at the age of 34. This must be the physical address where Jean and Will live at this time.

That same year my loving grandmother, Sarah Ellen Herrick Frazer, was born in Mount Vernon, Ohio as were her two older sisters, July 1, 1900.

Now a year later, Clarence has to resign as the president of the University of New Mexico on June 1, 1901 due to health concerns. His TB is not getting any better.

My Grandmother, Sarah at 5 months old, sitting on her Grandmother Sarah Colville's lap on December 14, 1900. Marjorie (left) is 2 yrs old and Beulah is 5 1/2 years old on the right.

Beulah, Marjorie and Sarah on their porch in Mount Vernon in 1902 just prior to leaving for New Mexico later that year.

The new century comes in with the bang but some trepidation.

3

NEW MEXICO COMES INTO THE PICTURE

This is home for the Herrick Family in 1902. Jean, Marjorie, my Grandmother Sarah, the short one, are standing next to Beulah who are both standing in front of their father, Will.

1902 was a busy year for William Herrick. He has three daughters in Ohio and a wife, and he is spending more and more time in New Mexico. I do not have any letters or correspondence from 1900 or 1901; maybe they were busy and close enough to each other that they didn't have to write for such a short period of their life. Mr. W. H. Herrick did a lot of traveling; his mailing addresses were Kelly, Socorro County, Tularosa, Otero County, San Antonio, and Magdalena. There are over 77 letters between the two of them this year. They spent a lot of time apart this year but the family did travel to New Mexico as the photograph attests to. As with any new family, finances are always a troubling and reoccurring problem.

March 27, 1902, Jean writes:

> "Dear Will: I am ready for bed except that I thought I must have a few minutes for you. Is it indeed only this morning that I watched your train whirl off as I walked off between the other cars over to Gay St.? I mailed the papers and letters to Charlie and letter to Uncle Albert. They came home and I'm not having had time enough to think what I should do first for our moving. I cleaned up the house. Then this p.m. went roaming a good deal arranged for our woman to clean out and country, and the boys to clean the carpet. Also arranged for having the Gasolem stove cleaned. Have done some ironing between spells. Now rain pours. I suppose you are nearing St. Louis. I am so glad I was smart enough to copy your paper of railroad connections. This evening Anna Schnebly told me Virgil's little sister has chickenpox. You know she was here playing with the kinder's Tuesday. I do not know whether she had it then or not. If ours should take it I fear it might delay our joining you in the country as we could not take it out to Mrs. Payne's children. Friday. You are about to leave Kansas City now I suppose. I hope you have had an interesting time in your long wait there. I hope too you had something hot to eat. There to vary the monotony of lunches. It still rains, quiet quietly but steadily and is warmer. You would be astonished to see what a change there is here since you went away yesterday morning. The yard and cow pasture back of us are beautifully green already. I would have gone

out home to clean this morning if it had been fair, instead I have just finished my ironing. I don't want to clean the house until it is both warmer and dryer so I can't wait. I think likely I can keep busy. We have not yet found a renter I have told number of people about it but have not yet advertised in paper. I must make up my mind whether to do that and do it tomorrow if at all. I don't know but I better. I fear that word cannot reach very far through private, on interested parties. It was several hours after you left yesterday before I could do good planning but after some cleaning up here my thoughts began to shape themselves into the proper plan for the next thing on the program. Saw Mable yesterday and she looked cheerful and pretty. I have not heard any news from the shop though I drove past there yesterday when looking for a man to clean the gasohire stove. Dave has come and is looking over my shoulder-very impolite to be sure. I must stop now. I think you know about how we are flourishing and I thought you would like to have a word soon after you get there. Makes it seem far away when I realize it takes so long to get a reply to a letter. I hope you and Alice will have satisfactory work in Albuquerque. Give my love to the folks. I think I shall mail this tonight expecting it to reach you next Tuesday about the time I fancy you will get there I hope you are cheerful my sweetheart. Jean"

Friday's letter from William, finds him in Kansas City making contacts for the harness business which he is in partnership with his brother-in-laws in Mount Vernon, The Park, Colville and Herrick Company, Manufacturers of Shafts, Poles and Carriage Gear Woods. Will finds the people here friendlier than he was expecting, it is a long way from Mount Vernon to New Mexico.

April 1, Will is in Magdalena, New Mexico finally and he writes his brother Clarence about his first arrival in Albuquerque. Clarence is in Mount Vernon at this time. He describes the arrival and his first day in Albuquerque. He is bothered about his true concept of the distance rather than direction of everything. He visits "Albuquerque's Old Town" with a professor at the university; it is quite an open walk between "Old Town" and the university. Clarence leaves for a trip in the South. Will stayed and packed household goods to help Alice. He gets more tired than he did at home, probably from the altitude. He figures that he will take the train to Socorro and from there to Magdalena and the Kelly Mine on the next day. Will's impression of the country is the deceptive distances. He thinks that if one had something to do and was well equipped it would be an interesting and enjoyable place. If one were here for their health alone and had nothing to do it would be unendurable, especially true of Albuquerque.

Three days later April 4, 1902, Will has made it to Magdalena. Jean is still in Mount Vernon. Will is helping Alice fix up the house in Magdalena. He gets too tired to work too long; he can only work half a day. The house was the only one available and it was that one or none. Its condition was deplorable but they are making progress.

April 6 William writes and asks if Clarence if he is moving into a crew house in Kelly. And Alice (Mrs. C. L. Herrick) is working on the house and trying to get it respectable. Clarence should be there the next day. Will climbs Magdalena Mountain and is surprised at the magnitude of the mountains. On the top of the mountain "the houses look like the smallest toy houses and the horses look like a caterpillar crawling along at a snail's pace."

One note: Will's and Jean's handwriting and its legibility sure seems to degrade as their relationship lengthens.

April 24, Will writes Clarence and they both seem to be in Kelly from the addresses. Will is working in the " Kelly Mine", but can only tolerate half days of work. Clarence is interested in the "Ida Hill" mine but is having difficulty in finding financial partners.

The Bogardus & Co. of Mount Vernon, Ohio, receives an acknowledgment that the transit of level replacement glass arrived "in good shape." Will adds a description of New Mexico and what the requirements of getting around and how pleasant a place it is. Dated May 6, 1902 and was mailed from Kelly, New Mexico.

On the same day, Will receives a letter from a friend of his at the Mount Vernon Machine Works, J. H. Brewer, Proprietor, and Manufacturer of the J. H. Brewer Centering Machine, General Jobbing and Repair

Work. J. H. Apologizes for not writing sooner after receiving Will's earlier letter. The rest of the letter is just about mutual friends and their activities and how Mount Vernon is changing so quickly.

Early Socorro showing the "Corpus Cristi Day" procession near the plaza.

The 6th of May has Will in Kelly, New Mexico writing the Bogardus & Company in Mount Vernon, Ohio about the glass for his level arrived in "good condition" and thanks them for the trouble they took in getting it to him.

Kelly N. M. May 6, 1902

Bogardus & Co.
  Mt Vernon O.
    Gentlemen:—
          The glass for my level came in good condition and is all right. I thank you for your trouble in the matter.
I find this a pleasant place to spend a vacation. There is so much room. The air is so clear that distances are very deceptive. On first arriving here one thinks he might easily walk to a mountain which proves to be thirty miles away. My first attempt at an ascent of the mountains was much the same. I expected to walk up in half an hour; but I was provided with a horse and found it took two hours of pretty steady climbing on the back

of the horse to reach my destination. People here seem to have very little regard for distances or the condition of the roads. My brother and I recently started on a 35 mile drive at 4:30 P.M. and drove at a trot even after it was too dark to see ahead of the horses down through deep gulches and over stony roads arriving at our destination a little before midnight. Recently two ladies made the same trip on horseback and returned the same way the second evening after.

The sun shines here with great power and persistantly except when the the monotony is varied by a sand storm which is so severe a horse will hardly face it.

Yours very truly
W. H. Herrick.

May 1902 finds the Herrick's, Will and Clarence busily involved in a project that takes them to Tularosa.

The letter on the 14th from Jean who is still Mount Vernon, to Will who is now in Tularosa, or Terrell County, New Mexico. Will has sent Piñon candy to the girls in Ohio and Jean says it looks like little gravel stones but after it softens up it was fairly good. She thinks he must be off on a surveying trip. Wonders where he will get his mail.

This letter was forwarded from Kelly to Tularosa, as was Jean's letter of May 24. In that letter from Jean to Will, the trip to Tularosa was a three day trip. She hopes he would feel better at the lower altitude. Will still has not gotten all of his strength back.

On May 27 Jean replies to a letter from Will that her search for the instruments and photo plate holders he is looking for are in "awful shape." She will look more.

By the end of the month on May 30, Jean is in Mount Vernon with questions regarding a possible trip of the family to New Mexico.

Early Socorro looking Northwest toward the School of Mines in the distant.

Socorro from the foothills looking east, toward the Rio Grande.

Las Cruces, New Mexico, June 5, 1902, William H. H. Llewellyn, District Attorney for Doña Ana, Grant, Sierra, Otero and Luna Counties, Third Judicial District, Dear Professor C. L. Herrick, Tularosa New Mexico, is setting up information and resources for their upcoming project. The closing of the letter states "Kindly remember me to your brother."

June 8, 1902, Will is in camp near Tularosa with Clarence and Mr. Llewellyn. They rode from the camp down the canyon to locate resources and water. They found a reservoir on the Mescalero Indian Reservation. Mr. Llewellyn thought he had a way to get the rights from the government. Will describes a range of bounds 25 or 30 miles west of Tularosa running north and south which they crossed to the east and saw the Great Plains of the White Sands. He thinks the range is called Sierra Blanca; one peak is 12,000 feet in elevation he believes. He says the planes of white sand is simply an enormous deposit of gypsum which has been ground into this snow white sand then was blown into dunes. At a distance it looks like a lake with whitecaps coming in.

The project in Tularosa was a large project that Clarence had landed and involved many influential people in the Territory of New Mexico. Clarence had a great knowledge of the terrain of the basin after conducting the geological and biological surveillance of the white sands region, as I mentioned earlier.

Jean in her letter of June 10 is looking at maps of New Mexico but cannot find the locations Will is writing about in his letters. She also was questioning whether he will return to Mount Vernon or if there is more work in New Mexico.

It appears that on June 21, 1902 Prof. C. L. Herrick was contacted by the chambers of Frank W. Parker, Associate Justice and Judge Third District, Department of Justice, Territory of New Mexico, Supreme

Court, in regards to the Tularosa Project. Clarence responds with a handwritten note on Wells Fargo & Company Express letterhead, with more boundaries of properties in question stated.

From June 22 through July 21 there are quite a few letters back and forth. Will is in New Mexico at Camp Rinconada Valley and Clarence is on a mining examination. Alice and her son Henry, are working with Will.

On 7 July, W. H. H. Llewellyn, responds to Clarence's letter to Judge Parker, from the Judge. He closes his letter; "with regards to yourself and your brother." Again it shows that Will is earning money but being away from his family is at a cost probably.

San Miguel Catholic Church, courtyard and Convent, Socorro.

Downtown Socorro looking east from the Plaza, early 1900s.

On July 13, 1902, William Llewellyn, sends Clarence the note written on H Shelton, American European plan, J. W. Fisher, proprietor, El Paso Texas, with itinerary plans of where he'll be with a second P.S. page with more information about researching the project.

On August 2, Will receives a letter from the Hendrick Manufacturing Company, Perforated Metals, General Sheet Ironwork, Cannondale, Pennsylvania. William G. Colville is one of Jean's first cousins. He is responding to Will's questions in regard to pumps in connection with the Tularosa irrigation project.

The letter on the next page is addressed to Prof. C. L. Herrick, Santa Fe, August 23, 1902, from Associate Justice Frank W. Parker, Supreme Court of New Mexico. The Judge is concerned that Clarence now wishes that he had not undertaken the survey of the irrigation enterprise. The Judge regrets mentioning anything about money or payments. He says, "I trust this explanation will be satisfactory for there is no one for whom I have a higher regard as a man and as a scientist than yourself."

JOSEPH F. BONHAM   WILLIAM H. H. LLEWELLYN

BONHAM & LLEWELLYN
ATTORNEYS AT LAW

WILLIAM H. H. LLEWELLYN
DISTRICT ATTORNEY FOR
DONA ANA, GRANT, SIERRA, OTERO AND LUNA COUNTIES
THIRD JUDICIAL DISTRICT
NEW MEXICO

TERMS OF COURT
LAS CRUCES FOR DONA ANA COUNTY
   FIRST MONDAYS IN APRIL AND OCTOBER
SILVER CITY FOR GRANT COUNTY
   FIRST MONDAYS IN MARCH AND SEPTEMBER
HILLSBORO FOR SIERRA COUNTY
   FOURTH MONDAYS IN MAY AND NOVEMBER
ALAMOGORDO FOR OTERO COUNTY
   FIRST MONDAYS IN MAY AND NOVEMBER
DEMING FOR LUNA COUNTY
   SECOND MONDAYS IN JUNE AND DECEMBER

Las Cruces, New Mexico, December, 4th. 1902.

Prof. C. L. Herrick,
        Magdalena, New Mexico.

Dear Sir:--

      In reply to your letter of the 26th ult. which came while I was away from home, beg to say that we would have had our first payment on the White Mountain Irrigation enterprise if we had of been able to file our maps in the Land Office as the parties required this from us. Under the regulations of the department your affadavits should have been written on the maps instead of being typewritten and attached as you made them. We have been compelled to have new maps made with room on same for your affadavit as well as the affadavit of the president of the company and we expect to mail you the maps today or tomorrow to be sworn to by you.

      In the mean time we have every assurance that the first payment will be made next week at Deming where Judge Parker and myself will both be attending court, and the Judge will then remit you your balance.

      We have been depending on you to take charge of the construction of these dams and if you can not devote all your time to same do you not think that you could get your brother to take immediate charge of the construction work and you have a sort of a general supervision over the work. Now a word as to your friend Cleveland, he writes me that his people are very much disgusted over their failure to secure the Cat Mt. mines and while he says that he is still working on the other propositions I am very much discouraged over the long delay. I am sorry that you have had to wait for your money. With best wishes I remain.

                            Sincerelly yours,

Dict.C.B.L.
                                  W H H Llewellyn

Supreme Court of New Mexico,
Santa Fe, New Mexico.

CHIEF JUSTICE.
    WILLIAM J. MILLS.
ASSOCIATE JUSTICES.
    JOHN R. McFIE.
    FRANK W. PARKER.
    B. S. BAKER.
    DANIEL H. McMILLAN.

Santa Fe, August 23rd., 1902.

Prof. C. L. Herrick,

My Dear Sir:-

I have your favor of the 19th, in which you state that you wish most heartily that you had not undertaken the survey of the Irrigation enterprise. My anxiety arises from the fact that perhaps something I may have said in some of my letters has led you to this feeling on your part. I wish to say that I have never intended to make any complaint of you or of your work in any particular. My last letter was written for the purpose of explaining to you the reasons why we were not more prompt in this matter of payment. In the first place it was my information that no money would be required until thirty days after the completion of the work. In our talks we had supposed that the total cost would not run over a few hundred dollars. This was the result of ignorance on our part for which you are in no way responsible, and I regret that I mentioned the fact that your bill was larger than was expected. But you will see the only idea I had in mind in so stating was to account to you for what otherwise would seem to be an inexcusable course in a business matter. I trust this explanation will be satisfactory for there is no one for whom I have a higher regard as a man and as a scientist than yourself. Will you please let me have the amount required to pay off your expenses of which you speak.

Yours very truly,

F. W. Parker

The Vigil Mill wheel near Socorro with ice and snow visible.

1902 finds 46 letters from Jean and 20 letters from Will; it's amazing how much love there is between these two. Such a long-distance romance is strengthened by all these letters. Clarence is a big help financially and morally. Work is rather haphazard and payment from contractors is like getting water from a stone.

The Flower Girls procession as part of the Corpus Cristi Day procession, at the Plaza, Socorro.

Jean's letter of October 24 is on Will's letterhead: W. H. Herrick, Architect, 115 E. Chestnut St., Mount Vernon, OH. Wills address is San Antonio, Socorro County, New Mexico and Jean is packing up their house to be able to move. Being an architect was something that I think Will had aspirations at one time to make his profession but he did not really follow through with, especially in regard to a license or schooling that would have made that possible.

W. H. HERRICK,
ARCHITECT,
115 East Chestnut St.

Oct 24

Mount Vernon, O., ~~Oct 22~~ 189 2

Dear Will —
 I was stopped here & now it is Friday suppertime & I must send you a line anyway so it will reach you Tuesday at least. Well my darling our goods — necessary things are off — they cost enough dear knows & there are half as many more

for the future. We
sent 1500 lbs
paid $38.85 for them.
Charles told me that
if the money was all
that stands in the
way he would furnish
the money & we could
carry out our original
plan. I was very
anxious after your
letter before the last
one for I feared to
send off the goods
till I knew you
felt sure you were
working for responsi-
ble people & would

W. H. HERRICK,
ARCHITECT,
115 East Chestnut St.

Mount Vernon, O., ... 189......

have the money for us
to go but after I rec'd
your letter Thurs. (yes-
terday) and found Mr.
E. had been there and
you were really at work
I concluded we would
risk it and go on with
our plans and then
if the money comes from
you all right and if
it don't accept C's
offer which is very
good of him, as he

always is. So I got
the 38.85 of him to-day
(They have to be prepaid —
household goods) Now we
are still planning to
go on Tues. the 28th
but have had some
talk of Wed. instead
& if it should be a
day later my boy
must not be disap-
pointed for I am
a day late all
round — I have to
go to Granville to-
morrow. I planned
for to-day but had

W. H. HERRICK,
ARCHITECT,
115 East Chestnut St.

Mount Vernon, O., ... 189

Too much to do but
most of all — the
baby was too sick
with her vaccinate —
She is on my lap
now but is better
& I hope all will
go off well now but
it takes my time.
I will not fail to
have you know just
when to look for us
but have no doubt it

will be either Tues. at
9:35 A. M. we will start
or Wed at 9:35 but
wont leave you in
doubt near the time.
In haste my love
J

About their earliest day in 1902, my grandmother, Sarah wrote:

> "I could hardly have any real memories in New Mexico but from an old picture of the house we lived in and oft-stories of that time I have such vivid pictures of the incident that happened there.... The house was like most New Mexico houses of that time, made of adobe bricks about 9 to 10 inches x 12 to 14 inches and perhaps 5 inches thick, made of mud with a little straw and dried in the sun. The flat roof had only a thick layer of dirt over the frame of heavy beams or vegas, with small beams or small trees called latillas across them to keep out the rain of which there was little. The floor inside was also dirt, sprinkled with water and tamp down. I believe this was an almost daily chore to keep the surface reasonably hard and thus dustless. There were two rooms and a link to for my parents, we three girls and a cousin my mother's nephew a young man about 19 or 20 who came along to help, to cook, eat, sleep and entertain ourselves or guests. Not a tree, flower or blade of grass around that little mud house, hardly distinguished from the bare ground around it. What a shock it was to my mother after the Green of Ohio, the neat framework brick houses and family and friends near. The house was in an open field near to the tiny town quarter of a mile west of us. There was a daily passenger train or occasional freight train with friendly crews who always return our frantic waving. I remember.... the tubs, pots and pans set around the room to catch the drips from the leaky roof the few times it rained.... My delight running down the field parallel with the railroad track pumping my arms shouting at the top of my voice "here comes the California Flyer!! And the time we were preparing to leave for a few days and my father brought in a rabbit he had shot and he moved parts of the pile of wood by the house so he could put the rabbit in the middle of the pile and then make sure there was a passageway between the logs just enough for our pet cat to get through to eat the rabbit so it would have food while we were gone" This note comes from Colville Family booklet that I have called: "The Colvilles of Mount Vernon Ohio – The long road to Irish and American frontiers, and what happened there"

It appears that in August, Jean and the girls were in New Mexico for there are no letters between her and Will.

The next letter I have is to Will in Magdalena on September 2 and its postmark is La Junta & Albuquerque Railroad Post Office and was written while they were sitting waiting for the train to Mount Vernon at the depot in Albuquerque.

By September 19, Will is back in Socorro till October 12 at which time he is receiving his mail in Metropolis, Illinois.

For a couple of weeks at the end of November and the beginning of December, Will is back in Socorro again. December 10th and the 26th letters finds Will in Metropolis, Illinois. Again for Christmas, Will is in Metropolis working with his brother-in-law's at the harness rigging company that they own.

The letter dated December 4 from William H. H. Llewellyn, confirms that with the payments to Clarence and with the maps filed with the land office and a final payment that will be made, the balances will be met. He and Judge Parker will both be attending court in Deming where Clarence can pick up the final payment. "We have been depending on you to take charge of the construction of these dams and if you cannot devote all your time to same do you think that you could get your brother to take immediate charge of the construction work and you have a sort of general supervision over the work." W. H. H. again apologizes for the delay in payment but "with best wishes I remain, sincerely yours."

1903 starts off with Bunny's letter dated February 2. There is no envelope with the letter from Jean; in the letter, she and Marjorie are with Jesse and Uncle Charlie in Mount Vernon. Jean and Will must be together at this time with Sarah, for there are no letters between them until September where Will's address is Magdalena, New Mexico.

On March 11, Professor C. L. Herrick, Magdalena, New Mexico, Mr. William H. H. Llewellyn, who is writing from the 35th Legislative Assembly, Santa Fe, Territory of New Mexico, is replying to Clarence's previous letter of the 3rd, as to paying off their indebtedness. Judge Parker and he will make good on the fact that Clarence has been paying interest on the money he has been using to cover this debt. See letter on next page.

Territory of New Mexico,
35th Legislative Assembly,
Santa Fe.

March 11,1903

Prof. C.L.Herrick.,
            Magdalena, N.M.

Dear Sir:

    Replying to yours of the 3rd, will say that do not wish you to make draft on me on15th,   I will not be at Las Cruces on that date.   I think we can pay off our indebtednes to you by that time.   Judge Parker is holding court in Silver City and I cannot begin to tell you how much we have both been disappointed and delayed by the repeated and broken promies of the parties we were dealing with.

    You shall be paid in the very near future if we have to go to the bank for our money.   And as you have been paying interest on money, we will make that part of it right with you.

                                   Yours truly,

The Territory of New Mexico, 35th Legislature, not bad.

SANTA FE
EATING HOUSE AND DINING CAR SYSTEM.
FRED HARVEY, MANAGER.
GENERAL OFFICE, UNION DEPOT ANNEX, KANSAS CITY, MO.
CHICAGO OFFICE, COR. 17TH STREET AND WENTWORTH AVE.

Albq — Aug 23 — 1903

Dear Mr Herrick;

I came here without the acts of the Company & hence, was unable to tell just the amount of your bill. Have arranged for payment of same at once and on receipt of its wish you to send a line to Hon. B.S. Baker, Albuquerque, N.M., stating the exact balance due you and by return mail you will receive same. Or should you prefer to have amount deposited to your credit it will be done at once and deposit slip sent you

On August 23 as you can read, Mr. (CL) Herrick receives this letter from William Llewellyn Attorney on very interesting letterhead.

Form 69

SANTA FE

EATING HOUSE AND DINING CAR SYSTEM.

FRED HARVEY, MANAGER.

GENERAL OFFICE, UNION DEPOT ANNEX, KANSAS CITY, MO.
CHICAGO OFFICE, COR. 17TH STREET AND WENTWORTH AVE.

2 190

from the Bond -
Trusting
that this will meet your
approval and again
expressing my regret
that you & I have been
in [illegible] I beg to
to [illegible] myself
Very truly yours,
W. H. H. Llewellyn

P.S. There will be no
necessity of you making
an additional affidavit
in the irrigation matter
& you can so advise
Mr. Griffith - We have the land
matter arranged satisfactorily,
L

Santa Fe Eating House and Dining Car System, Fred Harvey, Manager. His handwriting is very hard to read but most of it has to do with the development of the Tularosa irrigation project.

Again from William Llewellyn, on 24 August, it states the fact that he is directing Clarence's letter is being delivered to Mr. James D. Schuyler, Los Angeles, California.

WILLIAM H. H. LLEWELLYN,
ATTORNEY AT LAW.

DISTRICT ATTORNEY FOR
DOÑA ANA, OTERO, LUNA AND LINCOLN COUNTIES,
THIRD JUDICIAL DISTRICT
NEW MEXICO.

TERMS OF COURT.
LAS CRUCES FOR DOÑA ANA COUNTY
FIRST MONDAYS IN APRIL AND OCTOBER
ALAMOGORDO FOR OTERO COUNTY
FIRST MONDAYS IN MAY AND NOVEMBER
DEMING FOR LUNA COUNTY
SECOND MONDAYS IN JUNE AND DECEMBER
LINCOLN FOR LINCOLN COUNTY
FIRST MONDAYS IN MARCH AND SEPTEMBER

Las Cruces, New Mexico, Aug. 24, 1905.

Prof. C. L. Herrick,
    Magdalena, New Mexico.

Dear Sir:--

        By direction of the Major I hand you herewith letter from Mr. James D. Schuyler, Los Angeles, Calif.

        Yours truly,

        C H Llewellyn

1 encs.

"The Large and Small of it" was the title of this photo of Will, who was 6'4" and Jean, who is almost 5'4". This fuzzy photo was in an album of Marjorie's. It is hard to tell where this was taken. 1900–1905

This year is turning out much as last year did. Will is between Socorro and Metropolis and will be home for Christmas again this year? August 23 in a note to Clarence, William Llewellyn's note is on letterhead of James D. Schuyler, a Consulting Hydraulic Engineer.

JAMES D. SCHUYLER
401 Douglas Building
Los Angeles, California

CONSULTING HYDRAULIC ENGINEER
MEMBER AM. SOC. C. E.
MEMBER INST. C. E. OF LONDON
MEMBER TECH. SOC. OF PAC. COAST

Los Angeles, Cal.,
Augt. 21, 1903.

Major W.H.H. Llewellyn,
Las Cruces, N.M.

Dear Sir:-

By a recent issue of the Albuquerque Citizen I see that you are interested in the construction of a dam in Rinconada Canyon, 500 ft. long, 100 ft. high, to store water for irrigating 15,000 acres of land in Tularosa Valley N.M., the plant to cost $200,000., your organization being called the "White Mountain Land Irrigation Co".

Undoubtedly your plans have been prepared by competent engineers, but you may still desire to be doubly assured by the advice of a specialist in dam construction, and may wish them revised and reported upon. I have built many of the most notable dams in the west, and have a number now under construction in different parts of the country. Am permanently retained by several prominent corporations on annual salary to look after their hydraulic works, among these being the American Beet Sugar Co.; the Twin Falls Land & Water Co.; the Arkansas Valley Sugar Beet and Irrigated Land Co.; the Colorado Delta Canal Co.; the Central Irrigation Co. of California and others. I have recently returned from a trip to the Hawaiian Islands, where I was called to give my advice on the construction of a dam.

For general information regarding dam construction, I beg to refer you to my book "Reservoirs for Irrigation, Water Power and Domestic Water Supply" published by John Wiley & Sons, New York, which is in the hands of engineers all over the world.

special
This letter is not for the purpose of soliciting employment, but to invite correspondence and gather information about your work, which I may use in a forthcoming supplement to my book. I should be glad to know its dimensions and the character of structure proposed to be built. I have invariably been able to make suggestions of value whenever plans have been submitted to me, far exceeding the amount of my fees.

Yours sincerely,
Jas. D. Schuyler.
Vice-Pres. Am. Soc. Civil Engrs

On the 29th of August, 1903, from the Honorable Associate Justice, Benjamin S. Baker, Judge Second District, Department of Justice, Supreme Court, Territory of New Mexico, Prof. C. L. Herrick is being asked to clarify some of the billing questions in previous letters.

DISTRICT COURT,
Second District.
BENJAMIN S. BAKER, Judge,
Albuquerque, N. M.

DEPARTMENT OF JUSTICE.

SUPREME COURT,

Territory of New Mexico.

BENJAMIN S. BAKER,
Associate Justice.

Albuquerque, N. M., August 29,, 1903.

Prof. C. L. Herrick,
    Magdalena, N. M.

My dear Professor:

    Yours with itemized statement of account received. In your letter of the 24th, you say "The balance shown on my books is five hundred dollars, which I think is correct." In your letter of the 26th, you say "In replying to your favor, I am sending my bill as it appears on my books." You also say in your letter of the 24th, "This does not include a considerable amount of additional work", referring to the five hundred dollars. I don't understand the two letters, whether you are asking only five hundred dollars in full payment, as stated in your letter of the 24th, or whether you have amended your account. I wish you would kindly advise me at once. I will go to Santa Fe Monday morning and will not return until the latter part of the week, at which time I hope to have a full statement from you of the situation.

                                  Yours truly,

                                    B. S. Baker

William working on one of his many survey trips through New Mexico, both before Statehood and after.

Will with his survey crew, horses and wagon in front of their first Socorro Home, 1902–1905

Socorro, New Mexico, August 31, 1903. Mrs. C. L. Herrick (Alice) receives a letter from J. Baca. It appears that the Herrick's uses Mr. Baca as there provider of horses, tack, wagons and materials for their excursions in New Mexico.

Aug Socorro N.M.,
31st 1903

Mrs. C. L. Herrick,
Dear Mrs. Herrick

Find enclosed last months statement. it is plenty large to be sure $18.00 this month for water and we have had less than any month yet and I don't suppose we will even hear of any more this year unless it falls from above and that is going to make 4 cutting rather slim. Although it looks very much like rain just now. I am getting 3rd crop up very nicely still it has showered some on it

Have you written to Mr. Babcock about that Reaper or shall I write? I would like (if you want to dispose of it now) to take it out before putting 3rd crop in on top of it.

You will notice at the head of credit column cash from Byers I worked ½ day for him on his boiler and he

gave me $6.00 I havn't been able to
sell many grapes
    I expect you could kick me for
sending those grapes that morning by Ephraim
but they would of had to laid over till
next morning so I knew they would not
keep so very long and be good
    I saw Mr. H. at Church yesterday
but did not have much of a talk with him
he looked tired and worn out
    Mr. Byerts is very eager to sell
his land around here I believe if you
folk wanted it you could get a good bargain
he has even offer me to sell it to
you but I would not do a thing like
that if you would have me to look in to
thing and to how much land and and Ect.
for you I would gladly do it because I
would look in to it as a buyer not seller
    Hoping that this will find you and
Mr. Herrick well
        I am as ever yours truly
                B. Rice

This is the last letter I have to Clarence and it is from Harmon & Mathewson, No. 40 Wall Street, New York, dated October 10, 1903. The letter as you can read, again deals with the Tularosa Basin irrigation project which means that undoubtedly 1904 will be a good year for William's employment in New Mexico.

TELEPHONE
1610 MADISON SQUARE

BRANCH OFFICE.
N° 7 WATER ST. BOSTON, MASS.

The Hengen Investment Company
INCORPORATED.

OUR SPECIALTY:
HIGH GRADE DIVIDEND AND
PROSPECT STOCKS.

MINING STOCKS AND MINING INVESTMENTS.
N° 1135 BROADWAY.

G.B. HENGEN, PRESIDENT.
F.B. BOND, VICE-PRESIDENT
H.E. HENGEN, SECRETARY-TREASURER

New York, Oct. 10th, 1903.

Prof. C. L. Herrick,
    Socorro, N. M.

Dear Sir:—

    I am in receipt of yours of the 3d inst., and regret to note that you will not be able to undertake the engineering and superintending of our work. Do you not think that your brother could undertake the construction part of it, if you could give him the benefit of your advice, in regard to different matters? I should like very much to have you connected with the enterprise, because you have made a careful study of the work in hand, and are familiar with the local conditions. However, if you find that you cannot, under any conditions, take up the matter, will you be kind enough to give me the addres of some person who you think might serve our purpose?

    I am extremely sorry to note that you are not in good health, and trust that within a short time, you will have recovered sufficiently to enable you to give us the benefit of your services. Possibly we could so arrange matters that we could wait 30 or perhaps 60 days, in case you thought you could undertake the work then.

    In regard to handling some of your mining stock, will say that I am not in position to take on anything new, at this time. I

Herrick---2---

am largely interested in several mining deals which require most of my attention, and the financial conditions in the East are such now that it would be unwise to undertake anything new. Perhaps a little later on, I may serve you in this matter, if you do not make a deal elsewhere.

                      Yours very truly,

G. B. Hengen, President, of The Hengen Investment Company, Incorporated, on the same day, regrets that Clarence will not be able to undertake the engineering and supervision of the work but hopes that Will, his brother, will be able to on their take the construction part of it and is hoping that Clarence will be a consulting party. It also appears that this letter is in regard to Clarence's failing health at this time.

C. L. Herrick, Esquire, receives a letter dated November 16, in regard to inquiries as to good horse teams, plus equipment and semi-experienced help the can that can help Clarence with his work. I wish I could read his signature; it looks like Rich Stackpole, but I can't tell for sure due to the handwriting.

Then on November 28, 1903, Cousin Mildred C. Starr has written Uncle Will an interesting letter: "Dear Uncle Will, Just after Aunt Jean had left for Fairmont we received a telegram from C. L. Herrick to her which read as follows 'Stop all moves, indefinitive delay reported today.' We suppose you have a telegram to but sent you this at the same time. We will forward the original to add Jean. Very truly yours."

There's a short note from Frank K. Pratt, Attorney and Counselor at Law, 510 New York Life Building. It is in regard to common property owned by all three Herrick brothers and a tax liability.

> FRANK K. PRATT,
> ATTORNEY AND COUNSELLOR AT LAW.
> 510 NEW YORK LIFE
> BUILDING.
>
> TELEPHONE MAIN 10.
>
> Minneapolis, Minn., December 3, 1903.
>
> Mr. W. H. Herrick,
>
> Dear Sir:-
>
> Yours relating to the tax upon the lots held in common was duly received. The time for paying these taxes without penalty expired Oct. 31. Not hearing from you or either of the brothers, I did not know but you had remitted to the treasurer, direct. Since then, I have received checks from them. I have paid all of these taxes today, and your share of the common tax is $8.86. This at your request I pay out of the estate funds. The receipt for this tax I send to Clarence as the Senior partner.
>
> I paid all estate taxes, and the additional sum of $100. to Mrs. Hale to apply on her mortgage. When I have a little time, I will send another statement, including these items.
>
> Very Truly Yours,

The end of November and the beginning of December finds Jean and the girls in Fairmont, West Virginia, where she is visiting her old friend Beulah and is doing some library work for some of the libraries in the local area. By the letter dated December 10, William is planning to return to Metropolis, Illinois, but in a letter dated the 10th from Will in Socorro; he learns that Mr. Catron has gone to Kansas City to confer with Mr. Elmendorf regarding just when he and Clarence will be paid for the expenses they have already occurred. The stability trust of Kansas City is to secure an issue of $500,000 of bonds for the purpose of paying for the company and improving the property. This all has to do with the Tularosa basin irrigation project. The day before they took a ride but did not cross the river (Rio Grande) as intended because it was running with ice. There was a wagon abandoned in the river.

December 12. Will finds himself in Albuquerque on his way to the Metropolis, but by the 16th he has returned from New Mexico without getting paid and is disappointed in his dealings with the people involved in the project. He thinks perhaps he should have stayed and worked for Mr. Elton. Jean is still with the girls in West Virginia. On the 20th, will is working at the bending works. They are having difficulty with suppliers for the company and is having difficulty finding a place for Jean and the kids when they arrived from Mount Vernon.

December 24. Will has a found a house for the family, great. They will be together for Christmas. A second letter on the 24th, Will has forgotten to tell Jean how to get to the new house. Will must stay in Metropolis for at least a year, but his health deteriorates and he longs for the warmth and quiet of New Mexico.

Workmen are building the Adobes for the new Herrick house in Socorro.

Of the letters of 1904 that I have, the first one does not start till the late summer. Clarence's health has been deteriorating and on September 15, Dr. Clarence L. Herrick dies at the age of 46 from tuberculosis and is buried in the Socorro City Cemetery.

Will takes over his brothers surveying contracts and becomes the U. S. Deputy Mineral Surveyor until his death in 1921. He and Jean found the Security Title and Abstract Company in Socorro where Jean is the abstractor and Will continues the surveying and engineering.

Uncle Charlie Colville writes Will on October 14, 1904, on the letterhead of The Standard Gear Wood Company, office at Mount Vernon, Ohio, that he is sorry that Will and his family are leaving the bending works but hope they will find everything satisfactory in New Mexico. If Charlie doesn't get the dividends before they leave he will make sure that they get them in Ohio or New Mexico.

The Standard Gear Wood Company

OFFICE AT MT. VERNON, OHIO.

FACTORIES AT
STRUTHERS, Ohio.
ZANESVILLE, Ohio.
JUNCTION CITY, Ohio.
NEWARK, Ohio.
WELLINGTON, Ohio.
METROPOLIS, Ill.

Carriage Gear Woods in the White

October 14, 1904.

Dearest I will send this on to you this I guess will not need any answer as will see Robert soon all OK yet

W. H. Herrick,

Metropolis, Ill.

Dear Will:-

I have not had time to write you since coming home but sent you the balance of your first dividend several days ago. I hope it will be enough to keep you going until we are able to declare a dividend at Metropolis. Kindly let me know at once if you would like for me to send Jean some money. I am expecting to leave for Milwaukee to-night or to-morrow but Robert will take care of any correspondence which comes to me personally.

I hope you will find everything to your satisfaction in New Mexico and that I shall be able to visit you there some time in the not very distant future. Please let me know all about your arrangements when you have looked the field over. They will miss you very much at Metropolis but Bert Dalrymple will go down about the 25th to help Frank and I hope they may be able to get a good machine man to take your place.

Jim has written me asking me to take his place for ten days about the first of November and I have replied that I would do so from about the 25th of October to the 5th of November provided nothing intervenes which absolutely prevents my doing so. It will be very hard for me to get away but I suspect Jim needs the rest very much.

I have not heard from the Council meeting of last Monday night but hope the claim for water rent was abandoned. We expect Mother, Jessie and Jean on Tuesday. With best wishes to for you all I remain,

Very truly yours,

By October 29, Jean is still in Mount Vernon and Will is already back in Socorro. Jean is planning to join him.

In the letter of 7, November, Jean writes that she is preparing for the move to New Mexico, but is not well. Her brother, Dr. Robert Colville, has advised her that she will probably recover quicker in Mount Vernon than in New Mexico.

The letter of November 22 states that Jean's health is improving slowly. The Ohio families are getting ready for Thanksgiving. Will went to El Paso to meet with engineers and irrigators earlier in the month and got the "lay of the land" for surveys in that area.

Last letter of the year is from Jean, dated December 27, 1904. "There Will I'm going to begin my letter to you this morning while I lie on my back. I have been thinking about today as the day I was to start to New Mexico.... It has been hard to have all your delays with the surveying but there is no good thing it anyway and it." It is a 10 page letter about getting better, Christmas with the children and family.

You can see one of the girls in the doorway of their first home. The buggy is the family's main source of transportation.

The end of 1904, my Great Grandmother Jean, has made a diary of the summer travels accompanying my Great Grandfather Will. These were surveying trips to South and Central New Mexico with the three girls and others in the summers of 1905 in 1906. The diaries include entries from 1904 and the move to New Mexico in 1905.

Jean Herrick stayed in Mount Vernon, Ohio, until May 22, 1905, when she left to join her husband, Will, in Socorro. Jean and the three girls arrived by train in Socorro at 10:30 a.m., May 25th. They spent a week at a ranch one mile north of Socorro.

THE DIARY OF JEAN COLVILLE HERRICK 1904, Transcribed as best as we could for the hand writing was a little rough to read and interpret:

> From June to Sept. in Metropolis have had colored help. It was quite a task to find anybody but my washer woman. Mrs. Jefferson, exerted herself on my behalf and tried a number of people before she got one who would come. Aunt Airy—then her niece "Little Airy," then a cousin Prince—then a deaf sister-in-law Mrs. Tatum, who came and stayed by me thro the worst of my sickness—she seemed to be totally deaf but could understand a whisper if looking at you and knowing the general trend of thot (thought). When she was taken down with fever I had "Mary" and "Sally" for very short trials, but was glad they could not stay. Then Mrs. Jefferson got me "Edgar" true daughter of her mother Tommy. She is 17 and can do plain cooking and clean up the kitchen floor nicely, as well as, dishes—very quick and pleasant.

> Sept. 20, 1904 Sarah made a scratch on her leg and took down her stocking to examine it. The wind blowing on it made it feel better so she went out again. Presently I heard her at edge of back porch

standing with her stocking hanging down and calling again and again—a little louder each time "God! make de wind blow harder, Amen." The southern use of "done" seems very peculiar to me. i.e. "Has Mary done quit working for you?" "We has done eat our dinner." "Mrs. T. has done gone to Chicago"

Sarah, Four years old. July 1, 1904.

"1 can't eat any more," says Sarah, "I'm full." "How do you know you are full," Aunt Jessie asks, "Because I took a bite and it would not go down." Presently she asks for a drink of milk. Why, I thought you were full. What will you do with milk. "Oh it will go down the cracks."

Oct. 18, 1904. Left Metropolis for Mount Vernon to stay with my people until the Tues. after Xmas. Will has started for St. Louis the 16th, to go into New Mexico on excursion on the 18th.

1905

May 22, 1905. I spent the entire winter in Mount Vernon sick, but started for N. Mex. Monday, May 22, 1905, 8:30 a.m.

Reached Socorro, N.M., Thurs, May 25, at 10:30 a.m. Will met us at depot with tream and a spring wagon, and took us out to ranch 1 mile north of Socorro. We spent a week there and all came into town Friday morning June 2. Will and Arthur Devol started with the wagon to drive across the country to Sacramento Mts. I spent Friday, Saturday and Sunday at the hotel in Socorro, leaving the two children with Mrs. Hoffman. Beulah was not very well so instead of leaving her with Mrs. Hoffman and the children brought her to hotel Sunday. At 4 a.m. Monday morning I took her with me on the train to El Paso. We went over into Juarez that evening before time for train for Cloudcroft. Finally we left El Paso after waiting 3 hrs. for train from 7:30 to 10:30. We reached Alamogordo at 1 a.m. Will met us and took us out to their camp a mile out of town. We spent the night there and went on wagons next morning to La Lus (Luz) where we waited an hour for train up mountain while Will and Arthur drove on up wagon road. The ride up the mountain was remarkable, a slow hard climb about 3 hrs for 20 miles. It was hot down in valley and cold and rainy before we got up to the top. Jackets and flannels felt good. Beautiful views-road wound back and forth around the mountain like a snake. We reached Cloudcroft about noon. Will and Arthur came toiling up roads made slippery by rain and reached there about 5 o'clock. We spent the night there and the next day though still rainy left there 12:00 noon, the weather having cleared some. Will bought more supplies and hired a man and livery team at $3.50 a day to help us out to camp. Rain, slippery roads, hills and a tired team with a balky horse from livery delayed us. Our team had to help out livery team and we spent the night at Wim's (?) (? mark JCH) 6 mi. before we reached Jack Green's where we had hoped to get. The next morning the horse was still balky and after fooling away an hour we gave up. We stored that load there and went in with our own load. Will sent the man and team back and made the men who had gathered around laugh by telling him cheerily to "Give Mr. Smith, the livery man, his regards." We got to Jack Green's at 12 o'c. and were warmly welcomed by Mr. Green and his wife and Mr. Williams and wife - the latter had been there waiting for us for a week. It rained hard most of the p.m. and we spent the night there, but next morning pulled out in spite of prospect of rain. At noon we reached our first camp. It consisted of two old log cabins in Spring Canyon quite near north east corner of the Township. A man, his wife and two children named Sedgwick, were camping in best log cabin so we put up our tents and put some supplies under cover of other cabin. In eve. Mr. Green came out, after going back for our other load, brought Mr. and Mrs. Williams

Horses were a necessity of life in the 1900s.

June 2, Will and Arthur Devol started with the wagon to drive across country to the Sacramento Mountains. Four days later, Jean and their oldest daughter, Beulah, took the train to El Paso, then to Alamogordo and Cloudcroft where Will met them for the trip to the survey campsite.

> Next day the campers in other cabin moved on and we took possession of that place as it was so rainy and wet everywhere. The men began work that day Jun. 10, at the N.W. corner. They had a hard time to find it and ran only 1/2 mi. Sunday evening they took one tent and bedding, and evening when having done well they came to the corner near our camp at supper time. We slept there two nights, Mrs. Williams had a revolver under our heads and guns loaded on the floor at our heads. Next morning it was fair and we broke camp and were on our way about 6:30. We reached our new camp site about noon. Nice camp except that the nice clear water is about 1/4 mile away. A well of muddy soft water near and it serves for most purposes. Two brothers named Smith live here near us.

The men started out to work by 1:30, Wednesday, June 14. We are about 1 mile from South line and Southeast corner. We have had several days without rain. The work is rough, a great deal of timber, etc., but they have made about 2 miles a day so far. Our party consists of nine (6 men, 3 women) Mrs. Williams, Beulah and myself; Will, Arthur, Mr. Williams, Mr. Cook, Mr. York and Mr. Ritchie. The last three live here in the mountains and are Texans. The Smiths are Texans also, as are most, if not all the settlers here.

June 21. Last night as we sat round the camp fire Will and I were working and heard only snatches of the conversation, but were attracted by a bear story told by Mr. York which was something like this. He was going down a hill and saw a bear, he shot at him but gun did not work. "I thought I was a gonner sure" he said "but I told the dog to ketch him and I loaded the gun again, the dog held him till I shot him. I thought he was the biggest barr ever I see but when I got him killed he was nothing but a little old cub." Mr. York seems to me the most typical Texan and is very interesting. He is wrinkled and stooped, curls up the comer of is mouth and squints up one eye with a quizzical expression of good humor and drawls out his words with great deliberation. He is the oldest man of our party-pretty hard for one to tell much about age but I suppose he is fifty-has short brown curls all over his head.

We had a hail storm about noon. Some stones as large as a good-sized hazelnut. When it was over they lay on the ground an inch deep and Beulah and I gathered a basket, a six quart kettle and a big coffee pot full for clear water to cook with and coffee and Cream of Wheat for breakfast was much better for it. The men were some two miles west of us and had only a small amount of it. We sent mail by Mr. Smith's nephew and hope he will bring us some mail when he returns.

June 22. Young man told us Mr. Reynolds got our mail. Men got the work done which they wished to do from this camp and two of them went hunting for deer but they came back without any this a.m. Mr. Ritchie shot one but it ran away and they could out in leaf so thick it is very hard to keep track of deer.

June 23. Broke camp. Four men went with Will to survey west on the south line down to a place for new camp. They are about one mile south of our proposed camp. Mr. Cook packed load and with Mrs. Williams, Beulah and I started to the summit of the mountain where his house is. When we got near to his house on a little stony slope of road, Billy did not hold back well, and perhaps was a little scared and ran down Mr. Cook, who was, walking. Mr. Cook lost his footing and fell and was dragged a little way over the stones stopping when the team stopped behind the hind wheel. He was not hurt to amount to anything, but I felt pretty anxious for him for a moment. Billy frightens easily but is not hard to control unless something strikes his hind feet, then he will kick from fright, not from viciousness, I think. We got to Mr. Cook's about 10 o'clock and found Mrs. Cook and three hearty looking fat little children of six, four and 1 1/2 yrs. old. Mrs. Cook is little and dark-black hair, a soft slow drawl, and a sweet smile—a Texan. The two are opposites indeed. We had a good dinner good fresh butter and buttermilk, and venison which tasted very good indeed, especially so no doubt, because we had been without fresh meat for several days. I forgot to say that we met Mr. Reynolds on our way coming down to our camp with our long wished for mail and carrying a ten pound lard bucket of clabber and five pound one of sweet milk. We drank up all we could hold of the latter and took our mail. Then the old gentleman carried the clabber clear up to Mr. Cooks and left it there. After dinner Mr. Cook began to pack the horses and the fun and horror began. He took Kate first. She evidently had not been packed before and did not like it a little bit. She jerked away at first attempt to put the bed roll on her back and tore the skin off inside Beulah's hand in two or three places with the rope she held. Then I took rope. Mr. Cook got on one side and Mrs. Williams on the other and pulled rope tight around her to hold load. She seemed almost as if she would like to kick but did not, and they finished tied her out by the fence where she stood very uneasily all the time the others were being packed. The ropes evidently hurt her and she was uncomfortable until she got them off at our camp at night. Next came Billy and after seeing how little Kate liked it I dreaded to see him attempt Billy. I took the strap of his bridle from the porch as I had done Kate's rope but he pulled so hard on it I feared I was not going to be able to hold him though I hung on for the first pulling then Mr. Cook took the strap himself. Then his wife asked if she should not come out and hold him and she went out on the ground and held his bridle. Mr. Cook got the bed on his back and was packing other things in it letting ends fall on ground each side of the horse. Billy backed off some and managed to, went backward and hind feet smashed into box. Mrs. Cook held on to him until two skillets had rolled off and the bed roll dragged a good deal. They finally let go and she and horse ran together along the fence as if racing—both scared. Then she made for house and left the path to the horse while he ran into the gate and stopped. Mr. Cook then got him and brought him back to the porch, whipped him some and holding the bridle himself started again and gave it to his wife in a moment cautioning her harshly to stand at his side to hold him, not in front, put her hand out against side of his neck or shoulder to keep him off her if necessary. I thought she had held onto him very well considering and felt grieved to hear him scold her. He was very tired of course with it all and no doubt somewhat frightened for her as he feared when she was in front of him that he would get on her. After that he finished him with little more trouble—it scared him some when they drew the ropes up on him. He didn't mind them quite as much as Kate did, but when they hitched him out by Kate to the fence he shivered in a frightened way several times and then stood rather peacefully. Then Mr. Cook packed a staid slow old Dolly of his own with no trouble. Then a more fussy one but did not have any serious trouble with him. Then he brought out a Billy of his own which he said was "plumb gentle" and put his wife's side saddle on him for me to ride. Finally we were ready. Mr. Cook took the lead with Kate and Billy. Then Mr. Williams leading the scary bay with its bed roll decorated with the sheet iron camp stove on top and a dish pan and skillet over the rump-then came me on Billy no. 2 and behind Beulah leading the slow old mare, but he was so slow and Beulah so fearful straggling behind, that Mrs. Williams took her rope and lead the two while I brought up the rear and watched the packs to see when they were slipping too much. The pack with the stove on top had to be righted quite often and when we got not far from camp the bucket and canteen which had been tied on back of old Dolly on top the bedroll was dangling down under her. when I told Mr. Cook, he took them off and hung over his own shoulder for the rest of the trip. We had no serious mishaps in the five miles though some of the road was very bad indeed—would have been nearly impassable for a wagon. We crossed the Scot Abel River two or three times - my horse was very loath to enter and Mr. Cook lead him first time-after that he went alone tho reluctantly-he was indeed nice and gentle. After a time Mr. Cook said to turn Dolly loose behind the two he lead drive her so Mrs. Williams did so. I put Beulah on my horse after a time. She was very much afraid at first but got better and led her horse for a time. Then Mrs. Williams got on and rode Billy, and I led the pack horse and drove Dolly. We got through the trip and down to Scot Abel camp at 5 o'clock. Beautiful place—high log house with good roof and many cracks in the sides, two old wobbly homemade bedsteads and a table with the middle of three boards gone, a stove with about half enough pipe for it. There were bear holes in the steep rocky hill just back of house and the beautiful clear cold Scot Able River a few rods in front of us. On the other side of the river, the mountain rises abruptly. Wild strawberries grow along our path here and we gathered several handfuls.

June 24. This morning as Beulah did not eat her strawberries, I brought a handful home made a little short cake for her baking it in the top of a baking powder can. Last night, Mr. and Mrs. Williams slept on the rickety bedstead while Will and I carried the other one out doors and our bed on the floor for Beulah, Will and me. The other four slept outdoors on ground. This morning the men put up the tent we brought with us-or partly put it up while waiting a few minute for the bread for their lunches which

Mr. Williams was baking. The night before we left the Smith Canyon camp to come here, Mr. Smith was talking with us all evening. They tried to get him to tell a bear story but he said he did not want to start out, he wanted to hear some of the rest tell one and then he would tell a bigger one. They joked a good deal but told one, only Mr. Smith said the young man with them was at the spring and went away the other night and then half hour after went back again and a bear had been there and left tracks all round while he was gone, "Oh," Mr. Cook said "that wasn't no bear I was just round there in my stockin' feet." which of course was just teasing. Mr. Smith and made them laugh. While up there too we walked to edge of bluff near Mr. Smith's house where we could see mountains as far away as El Paso. They said on a clear day they could see the smoke stacks of El Paso with a field glass. From Mr. Cook's porch you can see off to a beautiful view to the South for miles and miles. Our ride down through the canyon with pack horses was beautiful but we could not take much time to look at it for watching the road and the packs in front. We are very much pleased with this camp anyway in spite of bad name everybody gave this part of the Township. It is wild enough to be sure but all the more interesting on that account. We are just at the mouth of the canyon where the Scot Abel flows into the Sacramento River. Mrs. Williams, Beulah and I walked down the few rods to the canyon through which the Sacramento River flows and found the road leading up to the later which is very pretty. We crossed the pole bridge to the flat place opposite us and retied our horses which were moved up in the bushes, giving them a drink first and while there, two men came up driving two cows with calves. The cows look wildly at us as if they had never seen a woman before. This is the canyon which Jack Green named Bug Scuffle from the difficult, rocky ascents. The Rincon is not far from here in which there is a rock which Lee Green named Bug Scuffle because it was so "slick it would make a bug scuffle to stand on it."

These are the accommodations that the travelers had during their trips across New Mexico in 1904-06.

June 26. Yesterday was a delightful day. Everybody was very tired Sat. night & glad they did not have to work the next day. Will and I got up at 5 O'clock and were off to a mountain 1/2 mile away to climb to the top of it to look for deer. We saw some fresh tracks but that was all. They had come home over that mountain the night before and saw a deer trail then and we hoped we might find the deer. It was a beautiful morning and the sun just touching the mountains as we walked down the Sacramento River. It was lovely and when we got up on top the mountain it came out in all its glory and we stayed there on the top to rest and enjoy ourselves a little before we started down. We got home a little after 7 o'clock just in time for breakfast, and we were quite ready for it too. Today Mrs. Williams and I have had a very busy day. We went up to Mrs. Meyer's for milk which Will and I engaged there yesterday for everyday while we are here. Mrs. Williams is baking and we have washed, mended etc. Now I am dressed clean as to my shirtwaist which I washed, dried and ironed out with hands only. It looks clean anyway and that is something to be thankful for. Mr. Ritchie has just come in from where they were at work and the unusual hour made me suspect something wrong. I saw he did not limp and his arms seemed all right, but when he came up I saw a white bandage around his head. He told us that while Mr. Cook was in a tree cutting out limbs with the ax, he sat down under the tree. Mr. Cook thinking he had gone in dropped the ax about 15 feet and it struck him in the forehead with the back of it. They washed it tied it up and at noon. A little later dressed it again and put pine gum on it. After dinner he walked home to lie down this p.m., and hope it will be out of danger tomorrow. Today when out at work Mr. York remarked "I can't imagine what God Almighty fixed this country for, couldn't a been for humans. Varmits I reckon." He was standing up on one of these ridges looking down over the deep canyons.

June 29. Yesterday the men expected to be only about 1/2 mile down the Sacramento at noon and Mrs. Williams, Beulah and I, took two coffee pots of coffee down there at noon to eat dinner with them. Mr. Williams just remarked that we might come down, but I do not suppose he expected us very much. We looked and looked but could see nothing of them. We ate our bread and meat and drank some of the coffee, picked a good many strawberries and sat under a thick pine during quite a shower for about 1/2 hour and got home at 2:30 p.m. We saw five surveyors running along down the river surveying the water for Oliver Lee who expects to buy up all the water along her I believe. We thot it somewhat amusing to carry a lot of coffee down there for our surveyors and not be able to see any sign of them, but be only a few steps from that other party of surveyor at noon. We ought to give them the coffee, but we did not dare. When the men came home night we learned that they crossed the river near 10 o'clock, and were over the mountain by dinner time. We felt sad over our wild goose chase after them. This morning however they started on their line just a short distance from camp and the first 1/4 corner on their line was up the canyon hardly 1/4 mile and on our road for the milk. We took our buckets and walked up there and watched. Soon saw them coming down the mountain and spent about an hour there watching them chain and set the 1/4 corner. I looked back through the instrument at Mr. York when Will set down there and forward at Mr. Cook for the next point. Then when Mr. York came up I took his Rod and held it while Will sighted back from the next point. Then we left them as they moved on up around the mountain and went to Mrs. Meyer's for the milk and picked up Mr. Cook's gun where he had left it for us as we came home. We are tired from yesterdays tramping. Beulah and I went both morning and evening for milk yesterday besides our walk down the mountain. I do not feel well and was glad to get down on the bed when we got home this a.m. We all went to sleep and did not get up until 11:30, then saw Mrs. Meyer coming with her two babies to see us. They ate dinner with us and went home soon after 2 o'clock. The children are fair and pretty, especially the baby boy. Mrs. Meyer is pretty too, with dark curling hair, gray-brown eyes and a fair smooth skin. She has the soft drawling voice of the Texan like Mrs. Cook. We have been buying milk, butter, buttermilk and eggs from her. She has not many of the latter but we had six for our dinner the other day and have 12 now to boil for the lunch for the men tomorrow. We hope they will enjoy them. They do not know yet that they are to have them. They came past the house just a few minutes ago at 3 0' clock having finished their second line and went up the South River to reach the Section corner 1/4 mile North of the 1/4 corner. We saw them set and will get a start in that mile yet tonight, and I trust there will be no doubt but they can get through here tomorrow night, if the weather is favorable. Then we will move Saturday.

July 5. We saw Mr. Meyer and Mr. Gillian start out to brake four, 2 year old, wild horses. They took them two at a time in a little round corral. Our men came past on their way to the corner, for their last mile down there. They spent half an hour watching the breaking of the last two horses. Next morning Mr. Cook brought down his Billy and Shorty. They managed to put all the packs on Kate and Billy, and Beulah and I rode Billy No.2. Mr. Williams rode Shorty. The men stopped to do 1/4 mile work near the head of the canyon, and left Mr. Cook to go on to his house with us and the pack horses. We got there about 11 o'clock and the other men came at 12 o'clock. We had dinner there and then went out to look at the view from the "jumping off" place south of Mr. Cook's house. It is a beautiful view over the deep Scot Abel where we had been and the mountains beyond, and far off over the plain and to the mountains near El Paso. We also a glimpse of mountains in old Mexico not so wide a view as some other places, Will says, but and Mr. Cook and family went down with us to our next camp near the head of Logan Canyon. We got here about 5 o'clock, and were nicely fixed before dark. We put so many fir branches under our bedding that it was as good as mattress and springs.

Sunday. Will was sick with headache and we did not do much but lie around until middle of the afternoon. We examined the timber near our camp and it is fine and it seems as if a 1/4 section here might be a good investment for the timber on it. We will look into it farther.

Gathering up everything to start again.

It takes a lot of equipment to be able to travel across New Mexico.

Monday we drove to Weed. Got off at 6:30 a.m. It is called 20 miles. Got there about 11:30. Did our errands, signed our papers, ate dinner and had horses fed at Mr. and Mrs. Williams and got away from town at 2:30 p.m. Dealt with Mr. J. D. Bunting at P.O. store and Mr. Bennett at the other store. We reached home at dusk, almost dark, about 7:45. Yesterday Mr. and Mrs. Williams, Beulah and Arthur went with the York's and Ritchie's to 4th of July picnic at the school house. Will and I spent the day at home and got a good start on the notes—did some figuring, Will worked some on the maps. We hauled a barrel of water, went hunting from 5:00 till near dark. We had a most glorious day together and slept best last night and got up feeling good. Will felt better than for some days. The rest days were a great benefit. Today they started out to run a line for Mr. Lewis along the creek first thing and then set some corners. Mr. Lewis warned us about the bears "Get them bears hemmed right smart and they will sure fight. Of all the poppin and slaverine of the brush they will sure do it." Bears pretty harmless ordinarily.

July 14. Yesterday the men were working over not far from Mr. Ritchie's house and Mrs. Williams, Beulah and I started over a short time before 9 o'clock and took dinner with Mrs. Ritchie and the three children. After dinner she and the children went with us on down the canyon to Mr. and Mrs. Farrel's to where their old people lived. The men were quite near the Farrel's at noon and the latter made them hand up their lunch packs and come into the house to a warm dinner of chicken pot pie, codfish, corn bread, sweet milk, buttermilk, coffee, cooked apples and peaches, lettuce, radishes and onions. The men were telling us of their good dinner at night. Mrs. Farrel is very friendly and talkative and amused me with her first remark. We asked where the line went through for Mrs. Ritchie was interested and expected it to go through nearly midway between their houses. "Oh," exclaimed the old lady "our men were away up there yellin' and hollerin' for them to bring their dinner when a little light man came a runnin' down over the hill right by our house and hollered at me that they were a goin' to cut our house right in two and then he went runnin' up the other side." Of course I recognized Mr. Cook skipping down over the mountain, like the deer, and going up on the opposite side of the canyon to get the point for Will's next sight. The Farrel's were sick before they came here but are well and hearty and fat now. They have traveled around a good deal and now she says they are content to stay up here in the wilderness and have good health and appetites.

July 18. Mr. Reynolds visited us Sunday and we listened to his talk with a good deal of pleasure. He talked about a bad tempered sorrel horse which he had seen kill a colt out here in the mountains in spite of all his efforts to beat him off with rocks. Then he added "when you see a sorrel horse with bald face, flaxen mane and tail and stockin' legs, look out, it's a bad breed, The devil is in the breed."

July 24. We moved from the camp in Logan Canyon last Wednesday. Mr. Cook moving us with his team and wagon while Mr. York took our team and wagon and went to Weed for supplies. The other four men went out and finished the last 1/4 mi. of the east boundary up to the north boundary, and did a little work for Mr. York as they went by and then 1/4 farther west. Thursday they began work down here south of Mr. Cook's and ran one mile where the rain drove them in. Friday it rained all day. Saturday it looked threatening part of the time but they did almost a days work before the rain stopped them again. Sunday it rained a good part of the day but in the p.m. When showery now and then Will got the horses, put Mr. York's old saddle on Kate with a gunny sack behind and Beulah and I rode her. Will rode Billy with a folded tarp roped on his back and a rope round his neck and over his nose for a bridle. We went over the mountain east of camp to the Mills place. I liked it very well, rode up the canyon and looked at the spring and the places to build. Then took shelter from the rain on the porch of the log cabin there until the worst of the rain was over. We then rode home down the canyon to the Agua Chiquita and up by Mr. Cook's which was about two mile round that way. It rained on us quite a little on the way home but we did not mind much and it was good to get out anyway. Today it has been raining every little while all day so they have not been able to work. Mr. Cook, Mr. Williams and Will finally started off with slickers and guns and have not yet returned. I wish they would kill some good game for us to eat, a turkey or a deer. We are all spoiling for something to do. Will and I keep busy all the time somehow for we have the notes to get into shape as well as the bumming (?) round whenever we have any chance. There are so many flowers here in the mountains. I would like to I try to press samples or draw them, but fear it would not pay. I will have to name them so far as I can anyway. I will give them the name of the Ohio flowers where they seem like them:

1. Crainsbill.

2. Tree cypress.

3. Spider wort.

4. Columbine.

5. Ox eye daisy like.

6. Another flower very like the daisy but smaller, a trifle coarser and branched.

7. Blue violets.

8. White violets.

9. White asters.

10. Purple asters large.

11. Three or four shades of a flower mustard from the light yellow to terra cotta and with two colors often in same flower head.

12. A blue bell, with long silver grass like leaves along the flower stem.

13. Several sizes of sun flowers or all yellow daisy.

14. A beautiful yellow flower with 4 petals and a leaf very like a dandelion. The flower is about 1 1/2 inches across when open.

15. A purple flower like lobelia, used medicinally as purgative, high flower stem.

16. Wild roses in profusion.

17. Black locust with beautiful cluster of lavender blossoms.

18. Bush with white flower very like scabra.

19. Bush with white flower something like flowering currant except in color, leaf something like locust.

Mr. Reynolds visited us Friday in the rain bringing two sour milk buckets. He ate dinner with us and made us laugh with many of his stories, especially one about a skunk. Said he had been waging war on them ever since one caught a hen and lots of chickens from him. When he took up a board in floor and went after it with his gun it perfumed him all over and nearly put out his eye. When his eye quit hurting he got mad and went under the floor and shot as long as the thing would move. At least a half dozen or more shots. He told it in his quaint language and amused us not a little.

Aug. 1. Mr. York amused us a good deal by some of his stories at breakfast this morning. When he was herding cattle "back east" in Texas he said, he picked out a brown horse he though would be a good one, but he said the boys laughed at him for taking that one. He said it did all right for a while until one night there was a terrible storm, thunder and lightening. The lightening would run over the cows horns till you would think they'd burn up and the cows got so scared they stampeded, broke out of the pen, 1600 of them. They got the rails fast on their horns and they carried them along between them, first one and then another. Some of them as much as eight miles, and in the morning you could have traced the cattle for a mile by the horns and pieces of flesh the cows lost on the way. Wal, that old brown horse couldn't see in the night at all "he'd run his head right into a big old cactus and stop stock still and stand there switchin' his tail." They did get the cattle rounded up all right that night.

Aug. 3. They finally finished the survey of the Sacramento Township on August 3.

Will paid off Mr. York and Mr. Ritchie and took Mr. Williams and Arthur a near ½ mile for Mr. Cook. Friday Will, Arthur and Mr. Williams went to do the work for Mr. Smith. Mrs. Williams, Beulah and I going along. We went in the wagon, Will driving and holding the instrument box over rough places and having his watch in overalls pocket. When we got to the Smith Canyon, just starting up it Will got out and immediately discovered that he had lost his watch. The men all walked clear back to camp looking for it but found no trace. They did the work for Mr. Smith in the p.m. for it was so near noon when we got up to his house that we got out the dinner and Mr. Smith had coffee for all. He had cooked new potatoes and other things for two old men who were stopping with him and for his nephew and himself. When we started home Mr. Smith gave each, that is each family, a deer hide and a fox hide. The latter however was shedding and not good for that reason. They would have been very pretty otherwise. Saturday Will and Mr. Cook laid up 15 longs for a cabin for us in Section10. Then Will paid Mr. Cook and we went to work on the notes Saturday. p.m. and Sunday. Toward night we walked up to the house sight in Section10.

The wagon train is on the move.

Aug. 7. Monday morning, we took the Williams and their things and some camp supplies over to Mr. Cook's. Then loaded up and the four of us started for Cloudcroft. Up on the summit at Dry Lake we stopped and took a look at the cave where several feet of snow still lay in the bottom of it. Just as we got back to the wagon to start on, having left Arthur at the cave for he was to go across country from there to set the closing corner on the north boundary, it began to rain. By the time we had gone a few rods and we were just entering the head a of dark canyon it was raining heavily and began to hail. We drove under large trees and got out and stood close to a large tree for shelter. When it slacked a little we started on all walking in the rain as we thought it better than riding and sitting in water on the seat. Will cut a stick to lock the hind wheels for the road was running & very slippery. We stopped many times & Will cleared the road of fallen trees-it took us about an hour to get down and we found Arthur soon after we got down and into Will's canyon. When we ate dinner it was still raining a little. Soon after dinner we got beyond the rain and it has not rained in the forenoon. The road was good and dry and we went sailing along in a trot. Spent the night at a logging camp with the Smiths, former owners of the mill at the camp. Got to Cloudcroft before noon, got Billy shod, had dinner and stared in soon after dinner. Had the roughest, wildest mountain road down I ever went over in a wagon, it was washed badly some places but had beautiful scenery and saw heavy clouds over the mountains behind us, but had no rain on us and we got down in safety with nothing broken but a seat fastening. One hind wheel was "dished" but that was started before that day. We reached La Luz about 6 o'clock. We got some new clothes, gauze, etc. and spent the night camping in Mr. Meyers' feed yard and shed. The next morning Will went to Alamogordo. Beulah did not feel well and I thought it best to keep her out of the sun so we did not go to Alamogordo. Will got back at noon and we got our load ready and had dinner at the hotel in La Lus (z), and then started on our way. We camped that night on the plains near an old man and dog on a ranch. The next night we spent at the tents of George Gilliland at his cattle ranch. He went with us ten miles the next morning to the gap in the San Andreas where he had a "tank" and thought maybe he would get Will to survey it. Will set up the instrument and could tell that he was on land that had never been surveyed and would it take a good deal of time to survey and decided not to do it. We got off our way somewhat after we left him and were on a new road. We did not get on as far as we should. When we found we must be off the road, we had to cut across the plains without any road to get to the Smith ranch. Will felt pretty certain of the distance. We got there and got water and then made our camp not far beyond it. The next day we drove well and made pretty good time and passed Bursum's well before dinner and reached San Antonio about 5 or 5:30 and talked some there and got meat and supplies for Sunday and then we drove a mile out and got our supper, fed the horses and started in for Socorro at 7 o'clock - the road was familiar and moonlit. We reached Socorro about 10 or 10:30 and our ranch at 11 o'c and were very thankful to tumble into the good beds there. Next morning we drove into town to Mrs. Hoffman's and found Marjorie and Sarah. They were dressed to drive to San Antonio with Mr. and Mrs. Hoffman, but were happy to go the ranch with us. We were very busy that week with notes and household duties and getting Beulah and Marjorie ready for school in one week. Monday noon we took dinner with Mrs. Hoffman and the children and leaving Beulah and Marjorie there, we then started for San Antonio again taking Sarah with us. We passed our old mud house two miles south of San Antonio and camped in the Bosque about two miles farther down. The next day had dinner in San Marcial. Camped there the next night along the river road and before noon reached the Toby Ranch where we inquired the way. We were sent through San Jose and got up on the mesa road and had dinner. Then went on to a Mexican goat ranch for water about 4 o'clock. We camped on the mesa beyond the goat ranch two or three miles. We trusted Kate with hobbles so she could get more grass. The next morning Will went out while I was getting breakfast. I looked around near the home near camp until he got a trail and then I waited, and looked, looked and waited, and planned until he returned about 2 o'clock, as near exhausted as he ever was I suppose and I ran to meet him with the canteen with what water was left. He sat by the road side and drank and then went on to the wagon and lay on the comfort and pillow I had under it. He rested before he told me very much or ate much. He had gone about 12 miles back and had water once when he stopped for 15 minutes to help a Mexican fix his wagon which had broken down. The Mexican had water and gave him a drink about 9 o'clock. About 3:30 p.m. we three started on foot for Cochillo, 4 miles away, taking what little water we had left and a can of tomatoes. We made our wants known to the first Mexicans we found in the village, got a man and a team, and finally got him started with his team, Will going with him for our wagon. They got back about 8 o'clock. Sarah had eaten a Mexican supper and when Will came he and I ate also. The next morning with a Mexican guide on horseback Will started with the horse of a deaf American blacksmith of the village. They rode 27 miles to Fairview where they overtook our horses apparently on their way to Arizona where Kate was born. They had rested all day at Mr. Scales' where Kate had been driven by Mr. Scales sometime ago. Mr. Scales told Will they had just left his place. When Will found them he went again to Mr. Scales' house and talked with Mr. and Mrs. Scales. They were very pleasant. Will hopes to see them again and have me meet them. He brought the horses back reaching Cochillo about 8:30 very tired and sore all over from the unaccustomed riding. I had cold water and sponged and rubbed his legs and back. He was in pretty fair condition the next morning to his surprise. The next morning we drove about 33 miles I suppose, for we camped just before dark about one mile from Hillsboro, Billy was pretty well tired out. The next morning being Sunday we could not find things very well but looked up the Postmaster when we got in and found him pleasant and got mail and information from him. We also a letter from Arthur telling us that he and Mr. and Mrs. Williams were out at the Hyler ranch in the Township to be subdivided, and that Mr. James Hyler would be a good man to consult about help. We drove out there, stopping to eat our lunch on the way out getting there about 1 or 2 o'clock. The Hyler brothers "Jim" and "Ray" were both away from home, and only Arthur, Mrs. Williams and the housekeeper of the ranch, Mrs. Mickler, were there. We unhitched harness and turned our horses into the corral and Will worked a little on his stadia rod while he waited for Mr. J. Hyler to come home. I heard the news from Mrs. Williams who was wildly delighted with the Hyler ranch and the wonderful hospitality they had received there. Will talked a few minutes with J. Hyler when he came home in the evening and spoke with a young man who came in there and whom J. Hyler said would be good help. We asked Mr. J. Hyler where we better camp and he said "right here" and we decided to make our first camp down by the river a few rods from their house. Will arranged to meet Mr. Hyler the next morning in town or on the road part way to town where he could find the southeast corner of the Township, and then go in and help him in finding his help. The Williams backed out of their bargain that evening Mr. Williams told Will that since his wife had such a nice place at the Hyler ranch to stay she did not care to work—but said they would work for high wages etc.

We felt pretty much disgusted with them for coming out there with the understanding of what their pay was to be and then say they will not work unless paid more. They did not need to come if they did not want to do so on the terms. I soon felt pretty well satisfied also that Mr. Williams had either intentionally, or unintentionally, passed himself off as the Head of the Surveying party. I felt that Mr. Williams made trouble for us through the whole stay in that Township, whether intentionally or not. We were very anxious to get through on that account as much as any other and so end the contract with them. We made only three different camping places and met very few people. Camped once near the grandfather of Jose A. Rascon and the latter came out to find out where the lines ran near their ranch and we found him a very pleasant intelligent and educated Mexicans. If he had not been out of town when we came and we had seen him at first he would probably have helped us in the work. If he could have found another Mexican as good as himself we would have had more pleasant work then, perhaps in spite of Mr. and Mrs. Williams..

The men stopped one day when it rained with Mr. Barnes and son-in-law Mr. Folgreen (Fulgreen, I thot) (grandma's phrase) and their wives and found them pleasant. Will was not able to finish the Township because the money appropriation gave out. We never camped up near the Barnes and Folgreen ranches as we had expected to do.

Oct. 3. They got through the field work except for some corners and odd jobs on the 3rd of October, and Will, Arthur and I camped in an adobe house on the Hyde ranch to finish our notes. We spent a week there, sent off the notes and then rested two days almost while Will continued the braking of bronco which he began while we worked on the notes. Then we started home across the country.

October 16. We left Hillsboro on Monday the 16th about 2 o'clock and reached home with our team, our horses and her colt, all in good shape on Friday night before 6 o'clock. No not home, but at Mrs. Hoffman's where we got Beulah and Marjorie and then came out home, getting here before it was entirely dark. The next day we cleaned up things up somewhat for Sunday and Arthur engaged board with Mrs. Hoffman and took his things in there Monday. Tuesday and Wednesday we both worked hard putting our house in order cleaning, etc., and Thursday we were both pretty tired and only did odd jobs. It was Marjorie's birthday and she was promoted to the 2nd grade.

Sarah after a little huffy spell with her sisters is ready to play and be amiable saying "I've got happyed-up again."

(Beulah) Mama don't you think it's time for Marjorie and Sarah to begin—I have washed all the dishes and half of the egg beater.

Sarah came in from play in the evening and threw herself down on her back on the lounge and picked up a sheet of paper upon which during the day sometime she had been doing some printing copied from a magazine. She looked at the paper intently for a little while as if reading a newspaper and then hurriedly scrambled from the lounge and rushed over to me saying "Mama, what does all that stuff spell?" With some explanation from her I discovered that it was the title of "Review of Reviews American Monthly." The letters were all there except the "i" in monthly, but some words ran left to right & some from right to left and some "any old way."

1906

May 18. 10:10 a.m. We left Socorro on trip to Roswell and camped about five miles east of the river on Carthage road at the Mexican goat ranch. We got off at 7:30 Saturday morning. The road was very sandy and we reached Guy Hill's ranch at about 2:30 in the afternoon in high winds and a few drops of rain. We found Mr. and Mrs. Babers there and they said we better camp for there was no water nearer than Wash Hale Ranch which is eight miles away, unless it came down from above. Jack Burton, who came on horseback, told us that if it rained even a surrey would bog down going over that road.

May 20. We reached Bursum's ranch, called Wash Hale place, at 12:30 Sunday afternoon. We camped there until Monday morning when we got off at seven o'clock. The view was beautiful back over the plain and the Magdalena's 75 or 80 miles away. It was a beautiful ride up the mountain to Jones Iron Camp eight miles away, which we reached about nine o'clock, then on 10 miles to Indian Tank a few miles into the plain east of the mountain by 12 o'clock, but there was no water. We camped a little beyond Indian Tank and started to Whiterocks at two o'clock and reached camp at that camp about 6:30 in the evening. Left camp at seven o'clock for town to get supplies and directions at 7:00 o'c.. Good hard road up the mountain but a great many roads, hard to find the right one- the one to Lincoln was the closest to the mountain -one to Capitan next, & farthest north, was our road, got on road to Lincoln for a little way, and found a ranch on hillside where America's told us how to cut across to our road even yet a confusing number of the roads for a while, but we did not loose ours. Took dinner out on plain. We stopped at a sheep ranch where there were two or three Mexican sheep herders and two families of white people in same house. The Block ranch was about seven miles away. We got there about 5 o'c.—quite a settlement of cottages of stone not in use anymore. Went in search for water about 1 mile & couple more too flat & camped in edge of grove. A man from the Block Ranch told us Roy acequia was 15 miles away. We left our camp a little before 7 o'clock and reached water near Roy acequia about 9 o'clock, and the ranch on the hill about half past. We saw a cowboy cook camp, a covered wagon with long wagon cover stretched out behind for shelter and two men sitting there. They told us it was 18 miles from there to Cedar Hill and we should camp there over night as there was no water from Cedar Hill to Roswell which is 35 miles away. Ate dinner under pine tree in a little rain and hail before we got hitched up and loaded. We soon left most of the timber. It had been beautiful drive with cedar and pinion most of way from the Block Ranch, up and down stony hills, but very pretty. Did not cook at noon & left noon camp about 1 o'c. We reached a ranch with windmill troughs, cattle and pigs, cords of cedar, and Mexican wood haulers, but an American ranch owner. We watered the horses about 2 o'clock and go on. They told us to camp about one mile before reaching Cedar Hill wherever we find a good place appears on flat place and we did so, reaching there about 4:30.

In the morning, Thursday planned to start about seven o'clock, but we could not find Kitty though Will had seen him when he started to hitch up the horses. We all tramped around a good ways round camp but could not find him and had to come in. Will told a man at Cedar Hill Ranch about him. We hope he may find his way to the ranch as it is hardly a mile from our camping place. There is good water there and we hope very much that Kitty may come and get some and stay until our return. We stopped about 12 o'clock on the plain and ate a cold lunch in sight of El Capitan Mountain which looked far away. We started on at one o'clock or little after. We reached "The Springs" a mile or two out of Roswell at 5:30. There is quite a lake there where stock water and it sends quite a body of water to the city for irrigation and stock. We had plenty of water once again and took a good wash and could not only wash dishes but rinse them. We all had a good sleep after our wash. We all put on clean clothes in the morning and all went to town. Robert rode Nan, leaving the covered wagon and tent there with Mouser staked out near them. We got mail and attended to business, got dinner at a The Roswell Hotel and then Robert rode Nan out to camp and brought in the load to The Capital Hotel which seemed more attractive than The Roswell. We took a drive Saturday afternoon to the famous apple orchards of Gov. Hagerman's father. It is a beautiful place and fine orchards. The trees looked healthy, had been bearing for 11 years. They spray them; paint the trunks where limbs have been sawed off. The ground looks nearly level around the trees, possibly a very little depression at the tree trunk, but looks as if they must flood all over. The very young trees have cane planted between them and well cultivated. Some of the older ones have alfalfa; some had nothing but pigs among them. We saw beautiful farms nearby with fine cottonwood trees for borders of fields and roads. There are a number of long stretches of our drive along road over which branches met. They were raking with two big mules pushing rakes and hay in front of them. They carried a big load and when unloading the mules backed away.

An old gentleman, at the barn and corral where our wagon and teams are kept, named Bradley has recently filed on claim at Alida says there is water and fine people. He is sure we would be pleased with the place so ought to see it. A man named White has store there and would be glad to show off the town. Mr. Bradley came to this country from Indiana but he came too late and his wife died with consumption, as did his 11 months old child who died two years later. He wants sister in Paducah, Ky., to come out and keep house for him. Roswell has about a half dozen churches, and elementary and high schools. It also has a military school. Mexicans live off by themselves and have their own school. It is a town full of Texans. We left Roswell Thursday between 4 and 5 o'clock,

May 31. The boys came Wednesday but one of the trunks did not come and we waited for it until afternoon Thursday. When it came and it had to be unpacked and our surplus stuff stored in Roswell and our wagons loaded for trip to camp. We drove out near the river for camp that night stopping near an artesian well and an acequia. There was good grass for horses, of which we now have five for Will bought a saddle pony in Roswell the day before. Left camp about 7 o'clock and before we reached the gate to what we supposed was Hagerman's pasture about 10 a.m. I think. We entered and drove some distance part of the way up hill which was somewhat rough and the area had some mesquite bushes. Took dinner away tho later and stared up the road which was going so much north that Will soon stopped the wagons, & took the saddle pony and rode two or three miles visiting two ranches. At the second one he found a man who knew the country and he laid out the road for him. He told Will how to get back to the proper road (which it seemed we had lost before we entered the pasture field) without retracing all of the way. We then turned round and found our way back to the right road and made 4 or 5 miles on it, I believe, before camping near the ranch house in Hagerman's pasture. Plenty of fairly good water. It was drizzling a little in the morning, but did not amount to much—made it messy getting and eating breakfast. We soon came to the red double gate out of the pasture field after we left the ranch, then a left hand road started out pretty well north of the east. We started to take it but after our experience of the day before we felt afraid of it even though Will had understood that after leaving the Hagerman pasture either of the two roads would reach what we wanted but the one to the left was the better road. The other seemed to be the main road so we took it. The difficulty was that we were to take a left hand road at the gate out of Hagerman pasture, which was said to be the 3rd gate but this gate was the 5th. I suppose they did not count the two gates nearest the ranch, for we learned afterwards that we could have taken this left hand road but it shows how easy it is to make a mistake in following and in giving directions. It was simply the gate into another pasture about the right distance we supposed from the Hagerman pasture that led us astray the day before. We passed an open storm water tank the middle of the morning where the water was low and not good and a cow mired on the side of it—our men tried hard to get her out but had not succeeded when we saw a cowboy coming herding cattle. They waited for him and he pulled her out with his horse and a rope over her horns. Our men had not dared turn her head and pull sideways as he did, for fear of hurting her. The poor thing would probably die, whether from being in the mire so long or from the bumped jaw she had. We drove on to the next open tank where the cowboy was taking the cattle, saying the water was good—some horses did not care much for it but some drank a very little. We had some sand most of the way from the Hagerman pasture, but did not get into the heavy sand until after dinner and had a long hard heavy pull all afternoon, nearly everybody walked most of the time. Will and I took turns driving. We overtook our freight wagons about two miles before we got out of the heavy sand. It took all our men and both teams to pull the wagons through the sand. We finally reached the Mescalero Spring and pulled out to the side in the shelter of the ridge a little and camped for the night. They unlocked the chuck box at the watering trough because Ed wanted to clean the rabbit they had killed. Will and I drove on to find our camping place. Next morning when ready to lock up the box padlock was gone and I suppose it lies on the road or hillside between the watering trough and our camp. That makes three things lost, I believe, my glove, then Kitty and now the padlock. Will and I discussed whether it would be well to stop there over Sunday, but the water was bad and we decided to go on. Started a littler after 7o'clock that morning. Reached the Walter Clark ranch near top of the ridge sometime near 10 o'clock I think.. We got water for ourselves but not for horses—also got a pound of butter, which was very good. We came out on the level of a seemingly endless plain immediately after leaving the ranch. We all began picking up bits of wood dropped by wood wagons and carried it in to where we camped for dinner. About the middle of the p.m. we came to little clear rain water puddles from a recent rain, and the horses enjoyed them and so did we. We reached the Four Lakes Ranch about 4 p.m. or soon after. Found Mr. Smith, the bookkeeper, who spends part of his time out here, and part of it in town. He is an old bachelor who drank hard in early life but does not drink at all now. A quiet, and apparently an odd man. Mrs. Dagget, the ranch woman, was not well at the time. Mrs. McBride, her only neighbor, lives four miles away, was with her. Mrs. McBride is German and very kind and friendly. I sat in the house and talked with them while the men put up the tents after

Will and I had gone with Mr. Smith to look at the place he had picked out for our camp. This lake, on the bank of which we are camped, is one of four which gives the ranch its name. This one is perhaps 1/4 mile long and 1/8 mile wide, part of it contains water and part is only a swamp with tall rushes and grass in it, and part is only dry white alkali ground or muddy alkali ground. The water is not fit to drink even for stock. Next to the swampy marsh there is a cluster of cottonwood trees in which stands the ranch house. Out from it, in both directions, small willow trees grow along the edge of the swamp. For a couple of rods at the end of this row of little willows, and a few steps from the last one, there is quite a broad open space of thick salt grass—in this grass plot stands our tent about three rods from the ranch house. The smell of the alkali lake and marsh is not very good sometimes, but not serious. We have found that we can get a little shade from these small willows and some good grass on one side. It is much better than glaring sunlight all day. I do not think we were wanted here very much on account of the children mostly, as they probably feared they would be troublesome. I think now, however, they are not so much afraid of us as they see the children do not get in the way, and the trouble is pretty much on our side as Mrs. Dagget has a little girl the age of Sarah who spends nearly all her time at our camp. She even takes part of her meals with us and would like to take them all I guess. She is the kind that "wants the center and the track around it" and so it is a relief when she stays home a little while now and then. I do not think she is of a particularly unpleasant disposition, but is spoiled, and being one small child among a great many cowboys has no doubt always had pretty much her own way and also been teased. When she plays with the children she is rough and doesn't seem to care if she hurts others. However, she doesn't want to be hurt herself, of course.

June 6. Will and the five boys started off about seven o'clock, Wednesday, June 6, for the south end of the work near the ranch called, on the map, Mallet Ranch. But the men here call it "High Lonesome." I felt that it would be "high lonesome" here even more than after they were gone. I went to work straightening things up around camp when their wagons were out of sight.

June 10. This now is Sunday and it seems a long time since they left, I hope they may spend Sunday two weeks from to-day here anyway. I don't seem to have much to show for the time since they went away. It takes me a good deal too long to get the things cooked on the camp fire, as well as, to do anything I have to do. Have washed some and written some letters and spent a pretty sick day yesterday after a night of bowel trouble and exceptionally severe pain. The children each wrote a little in the 'home' letters yesterday and Mr. Smith starts for Roswell today, June 10.

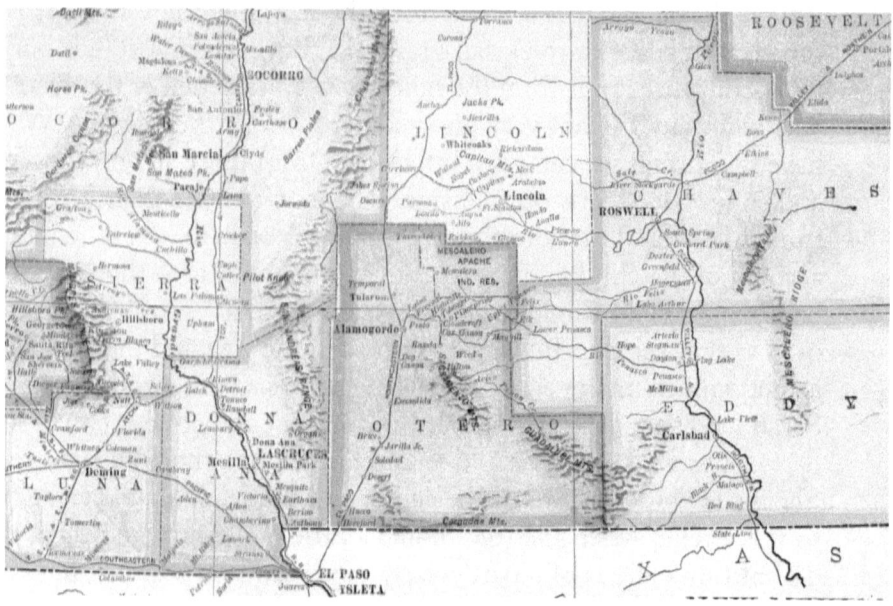

A 1904 map of Territorial New Mexico and there are no roads just the location of cities, towns and villages. The railroads, major rivers, arroyos and the general area of mountains are shown but if you were not on the train your travels were as the land and terrain allowed. Being a well traveled surveyor in New Mexico, Will would have known the best routes for horses, wagons and people. They likely would have traveled the Rio Grande and other rivers and the train routes for the "Camino Real" had been traveled for more than 400 years. There was abundant food and water for the horses and the route was better suited for wagons. When crossing large open areas away from the major river valleys and trails,

Will's knowledge of the terrain made a journey of this magnitude relatively easy and practical, for the day.

June 14. Mr. Smith did not start to Roswell until Monday afternoon, June 11. I was sick Sunday night and Monday again but got better in the afternoon and on Tuesday washed. I did not begin very early and it took me until afternoon to finish, but I had a big washing and did them well. I had about seven dozen pieces so though it took me a big half day to do them I would be making pretty good wages as a wash woman at 35 cents per dozen (as the woman charged in Roswell) I don't think I could stand it? It used me up even though I could stick right to it with energy until it was done. I ached and I suppose took cold that night. I have been pretty miserable ever since. I baked light bread in the range at Mrs. Dagget"s yesterday and ironed a few pieces while there, also ironed a little today again. Think I will have to let the children wear most of their ginghams unironed here after this for it is too hard for me to do it, and I hate very much to go to the ranch to do it. Mrs. Dagget says it is no bother to her, but I don't like to do it.

June 17. Friday Mrs. Daggett sent for me in the morning and I went up and did her work and rubbed her legs and bathed her feet. I got dinner for the children then for her and me, then about three for the men who were off horse hunting. One of theirs came home with a little mustang, a cute looking little wild thing but with a swollen front foot, and had a Devil head in it the boy said. About five o'clock I boiled a little potato for yeast and Mr. Dagget and Mr. Purcell (Mrs. Dagget's father) came home, and to leave her own people to take charge of Mrs. Daggett and the ranch. I sent Zula home for her supper because I felt I was too tired to be bothered with her. Her father and grandfather could take care of her. Saturday I baked four very nice loaves of bread and gave two loaves to Mrs. Dagget. I am to make up her bread tomorrow morning and she will let me have two of hers. I was very tired when I got through baking and ironing a waist for myself and dress for Marjorie. I rested a little while, took a bath, and then we got supper frying some fresh liver from a beef they butchered at the ranch. I hardly dared hope Will would come home but watched a little for him all the time I was getting supper. Just when it was done we saw him coming,-Beulah getting the first glimpse. We all ran up to the watering trough to meet him and when the horses got through drinking all got in the wagon and rode down to camp. I helped unhitch and then we set the skillet of liver on again, and then had our nice fresh bread and liver. Will and I had so much to say we could not get done for a time after we got to bed. We got up about 4:30 this morning and got our breakfast and took the ponies to water for they came round to us to ask for water and breakfast. It was cute to see them coming straight around the salt and come up near us when we had just finished our own breakfast and they looked at us. When the children got up I cooked their breakfast and then combed Marjorie's and Sarah's hair. Then Will and I looked over all the notes for the boundaries for a few miles of subdivisions. They had finished the first Township, except one mile in 8 1/2 days. We are delighted. If they get on that well all the time we will get through before cold weather. After getting supplies for camp, we spread out beds got clean clothes for Will, etc. Then it was 11 o'clock and we began dinner—had nice tender fresh steak from the ranch, and milk with fresh light bread & Will said it was the best dinner he would have for some days. At a few minutes before 1 o'clock he told us goodbye and we watched him out of sight. He won't be back again for two weeks I suppose now. The boys will be disappointed that he brings no mail for no one has brought any from town. Mr. White came out in an auto on Saturday and stopped a little while then went on but he brought no mail for anybody. I think likely Mr. Smith will be back soon or certainly will send the mail with someone this week. He told me he would send it out if he did come out himself. Mr. Smith came Monday afternoon. I read a letter from Dougherty containing the Elemendorf money (of long standing.) On Monday I baked light bread, Tuesday and Wednesday at the ranch, for a barbecue to be held June 29 and 30 because of the primary election on June 30, Mr. White being a candidate. Friday noon Ed Roberts came to Four Lakes while the men were out at work and worked until noon then drove to Four Lakes getting there at supper time. He was tired and dusty. We all had barbecue supper there Friday night and Saturday morning for breakfast. We had barbecue meat and light bread from there for our camp. We spent Saturday resting, doing odd jobs, writing letters, etc.

Sunday morning July 1, the boys went out to camp with the wagon and in the afternoon, after eating dinner with Mrs. Dagget. Will and I went out with the Spring Wagon and the children. We camped near Scott and Frier's place that night, also on Monday and Tuesday, getting a soaking rain Monday night.

Then on Wednesday, July 4, we moved to Mr. Arizona's. It rained a good part of time from Thursday noon until Sunday. The rain tapered off a little while Saturday afternoon. There were showers all the week following but many of them went round. It rained a very little at the house in the daytime, sometimes hitting the men out a work, but only for a short time and they worked right on doing a good weeks work. They had finally finished the 3rd Township the next day after we got to Mr. Arizona's, just before the rain set in. They were getting pretty wet setting the last corners that day, July 5.

July 6, Mr. Arizona building fire in fireplace on rainy day, speaking of fuel, said he had been using some wood left from last winter for he had been so busy "pullin' out bogs" from the lakes he had not had time to haul any "chips." He was speaking about Ed not liking to cook meals for chance passersby, he said "The cook was roarin' and beef'n 'around about it." At Mr. Anderson's he was speaking of the stove not baking well on bottom. Mr. Newman said Mr. Anderson said "The woman always gets cut up about it not baking." They got to work a little the afternoon of July 7 and made three miles. They worked a little on Sunday the 8th because they were so glad to get out. We moved away from there on July 20.

July 23. Then yesterday they finished the 5th Township. We are camping here in the house at Anderson's where Mr. Newman cooks in the house & I write my notes sitting in a rocking chair. I baked some light bread today. Mr. Newman sleeps in the house with the two Anderson boys while Walter, Ned, Kenneth and Robert have a tent, and Will and I and the children have a tent. We have not had any rain here so far though there were some showers in the distance just after we got here, and they had been having heavy rains before we came. We have been very fortunate so far, only one soaking.

August 13. There was a Roundup at Four Lakes. We take the whole day to see all we can of it, and to celebrate Will's birthday. We had a fine day.

August 15. Have just been over to one of the Roundup wagons nearest the ranch where Mr. McIntosh is the cook. He tells me of his life, he was born in 1841 in the Creek tribe, captured by the Crow tribe of Indians when he was five years old. He was out riding a pony like Sarah and Zula were this morning. He said he never had pants on until he was 20 years old. He served in the army with Custer until last battle when he told Custer that the man who "ran" that day would live the next. He tried to get Custer not to fight. They fought and Mr. McIntosh watched from a hill in the distance he said, and only he, Curly the Crow," as he is called, lived to tell the tale. Mr. McIntosh says he has a ranch not far from Yellowstone Park. He wants to have it surveyed before long and start a beet sugar factory. He told me he would send me the Custer book which tells of his life, but said when I read it not to feel that it is really his life, for he said he was no hero, and while it was meant to represent him, it was not really like him.

August 22. We left Four Lakes and came to Ranger Lake to camp in the 9th Township. I took the little girls to Mrs. McBride' before we came out here, and have not seen them since and this is August 31. We thought, Will and I, might drive back to Four Lakes next Sunday, but as the mail is not likely to be there for a day or two later and no freight, that we may not go. The first day the men worked in the south Township above here they did not get back until nearly 8 o'clock. I got very uneasy lest they should miss their way in the dark and have to spend the night out without supper, but they had the cow trails to follow after it got dark.

August 25. They had their first serious accident. Jimmy fell with Kenneth, turning a complete somersault and breaking his neck & dying instantly. Kenneth was entirely unhurt. We were so thankful for what seemed and almost miraculous escape for Kenneth that we did not feel quite so bad over the horse, and yet my heart ached to think of the gentle little pet of the camp being killed. Yet I was glad he was killed instantly instead of being crippled and suffering. He was so cute so good natured that everybody petted him.

Send to Mrs. Daggett from Socorro.

Head ache medicine

Bloomer pattern

Seeds from Mount Vernon of little fine vine, any other seeds I find she would like.

Send Ed new - Ben Hur.

NOTE: Tho, thot, and & are as used by Jean C. Herrick. I tried to spell as she did but did change a few words and added a few commas. Most of the (words or phases) are mine Jfs. This in the end of the Diary. Jfs is my Mother.

A dry river bed or Arroyo as they are called in New Mexico. What a contrast for the Herrick's who were from green Ohio and the East.

Cool refreshing water from a clean source.
When in the wilderness one makes the best of what is available.

A very interesting man-made structure visible across from the horse and buggy. The print is from a large glass negative.

May 11, 1905, C. Judson Herrick was a Professor in the Department of Zoology, Denison University Granville, Ohio, writes in regard to Clarence's death:

> My Dear Jean:
>
> I am sending this to Mount Vernon, though I do not know whether it will find you there. I enclose the last October tax receipt recently received from Uncle Albert. I believe that you have filed the others.
>
> Regarding the Journal of Neurology and Bulletins of which you

write in your letter of the 5th, if you and Will care to part with these, they will be of greatest value to us. They may, if fortune favors us, and a blessed to complete several sets, as we are short only very few copies in several sets. The geology survey and pamphlets will also be of great value, and any other scientific literature, for we lost everything. If among your collections you can pick up any copies of state geological or other scientific papers, they will be very welcome.

We shall be anxious to hear from you as soon as you reach the Territory how you stood the trip and all the other news. I trust that you continue to gain. We are in about the usual state of chronic disorder. Pretty well in general, though Ruth has just lost a week of school with the pinkeye and now Mary has it and suffers a general demoralization in consequence. But none of these things are serious.

As ever, sincerely yours,

C. Judson Herrick

A "Night Message" Western Union telegraph arrives for Will in Socorro, from Jean in Mount Vernon. I gather she is getting ready to board the train for Socorro.

The letters that follow are letters written in conjunction with the "Diary."

Thursday, May 25, 1905, at 10:30 a.m., Jean, Beulah, Marjorie, and Sarah reach Socorro, New Mexico. They left Mount Vernon May 22, so it only took four days to travel on the train from Mount Vernon to Socorro as the "Diary" explains.

Horse Spring, New Mexico.

Jean's July 28 letter to the folks in Ohio, is from Camp five, Sacramento Mountains. She talks about the rain, the wet beds, the lack of sun and mail. Their mail comes to Weed, New Mexico, and then brought up to the camp. There is a post office at Wright, New Mexico were the children in the area go to school. Jean talks about the beautiful purple flowers that grow in the canyon and are almost as high as some flowers. When the surveying is finished in that location they will go directly to Hillsboro, New Mexico.

August 8, Jean's letters from Cloudcroft, New Mexico to the folks again in Mount Vernon. They stopped in a sawmill camp and slept in real beds for the first time in two months. Will strained his back and was very lame for several days. They have had several days of heavy rain and there is flooding all around. The hotel man says the cottages there were "plumb full."

On the 29th of November, 1905 William H. Herrick, Esq. received a letter from Robert J. Terry at the Office of Dougherty & Griffith Attorneys at Law in Socorro, in regard to alfalfa that Will and Jean have for sale. In the notes that Jean writes on the letter from Mr. Terry, the Mrs. H. that is mentioned is probably Mrs. Hilton.

December 1 finds Jean in Socorro selling alfalfa and other things. There was a package of "Live Stock Bill of Sale "receipts in my collection and she discusses other financial matters and corrections to notes with Will, who is still in Cloudcroft.

There are 34 letters between Will and Jean while they are separated early in the year between New Mexico and Ohio.

I only have one letter from 1906, but it reminds me of modern day junk mail, dated November 19 from the Home Kindergarten School, Detroit, Michigan, trying to get Jane to buy their magazine where you can try it for one week for a dollar and "will be under no obligation whatsoever," to continue after receiving the trial month. Yours sincerely, Carrie C. Varney. Does this sound like junk mail? Jean and Will must've been together for this year due to the lack of letters.

Someone was pretty good about archiving all this personal stuff. There is a receipt from the El Capitan Hotel in Roswell, New Mexico, payable to Mrs. Anna C. Herrick, Will's mother, for $948.00, May 28th.

ONE BLOCK WEST OF DEPOT
NEWLY FURNISHED....

ON THE EUROPEAN PLAN
....NEWLY BUILT

El Capitan Hotel

R. L. MILLER, Prop.

Meals 25 cts.
Two in Room 70 cts.
Single Rooms 50 cts.
Weekly Rates / Single $7.00
Room & Board | Double $12.00

Roswell, N. M., *May 28* 190*6*

For Value received I promise to pay on demand to Anna C. Herrick Nine hundred and fourty eight and %od ($948⁰⁰) dollars

The first letter of 1907

Will's address is Mr. W. H. Herrick, Central, N.M Socorro March 26 7 PM 1907 and is postmarked Central New Mexico March 28, 1907. Jean writes that she has just returned from "poor little" Mrs. Crabtree's home who passed away about noon today, April 3. She says "I had not been out since Sunday and had no intention to go out today but where Mrs. Hoffman telephone to see how I felt." So I guess by 1907 they have a telephone in their house. "Sarah was not really well and I kept her out of school the day of as I went away right after dinner. It is Thursday morning now and cold and windy." Construction thoughts and details as well as choral practice which takes up time."I would like to cut. Maybe I will. My, how the wind blows, etc. houses I like. I hope it is not hindering your work."Thursday evening, Jean has returned from the services for Mrs. Crabtree. Jean and the rest of her friends understand that Mr. Crabtree will be going with the body to Albuquerque on the train. The last part of the letter has to do with well-to-do people not doing or thinking of what is supposed to be done on how long it takes to get anything done, month after month. All replies seem interminable. Even in those days, you could tell who was where by what horse was parked outside of that house. Signed "Good day My Dearest."

A handwritten envelope for Mrs. W. H. Herrick, Socorro, New Mexico, to Mr. W. H. Herrick, Central, N. M. The Central, N.M. post office must be the single post office that covers both Magdalena and Kelly. This type letter is a great window into life in a western town with a postscript that refers to timber scribe to be used in the new house construction. March 26, 1907.

The surprise of this envelope is the fact that there are two letters in it. Jean's letter is one of the few typed letters that I have between Jean and Will is as follows:

Socorro, N. M. Mar. 31, 1907.

Dear Will;-

I am"ausgespielt" to-day after the Easter service; I was really done out when I got to bed last night after our last choir practice but I revived to get through with the service this morning but I am powerful glad I do not have to go to church to-night. The program went off in good shape to-day and our music went well. Mrs. Twining had a duet picked from the S.S.Easter program for Mrs. Newcomb and me to sing which was very pretty and we got throgh that all right. My only criticism on the program as a whole was that it lacked spirituality. The music was pretty, the pieces appropriate and everything went without a hitch but there was not a prayer or verse of the Bible given and it did not seem quite right to me. Mrs. Hilton of San Antonio is visiting Mrs. Bursum and was at church to-day. She is to be here two or three weeks she says I would like to have her here at our house but if she is here that long I want to have her when you are home. My! but I hope you are through the main part of the work to-day or nearly so at least. * wish I knew but I suppose I will hear Tuesday anyway. Yes your"add" was in the Albuquercue paper. I seem to have a fever to-day my head is burning and my hands and feet cold and chills run over me and my head aches but I will be all right to-morrow I suspect when I get a good nights sleep I did not sleep much last night. A letter from Charlie says
as Prof.of Neurolirgy
he is going to Chicago. He also writes something on money business which I think I will leave until you come home, he was just starting to Wis. to a Naturalists meeting. He also said that Laura is not so well again and that he fears she will never be any better.

I hope we will see you soon Dearest
Jean

I will enclose a letter Marjorie wrote in school

The second letter is from Marjorie, Will and Jean's middle daughter.

> Socorro N. Mex.
> March 27, 1907.
>
> Language
>
> Dear Papa,
>
> When are you coming home? Mamma got your letter yesterday. She hoped that you would be home next Sunday but she found in your letter that you would not come home till the Sunday after next.
>
> We miss you very much and will all be glad when you come home.
>
> Since sister will soon hear our language I will stop.
>
> Your loving daughter,
> Marjorie.

As you have read, Marjorie is looking forward to having her father home.

August 14, 1907, Will is excited about a dividend that Charles had mentioned but did not realize it was going to be anything like this. He is sending money to the bank as a deposit so that they can pay off some bills that they have and just make life run better. They still have a rather large note in Mount Vernon but can pay it down. He also writes that he is in contact with the examiner in relationship to his U. S. Deputy Mineral Surveyors certifications. He has also written to Walter and talked with Mr. Brown over the telephone and all the work that they had talked about he still wants done. Will has been feeling pretty well, a few headaches in the morning but beautiful weather. He says he has been taking "Polaris Observations" on Monday night will do it again tonight. These observations should help with a claim he is working on.

It seems that being a US Deputy mineral surveyor has brought Will considerable work. This letter of August 18, 1907, finds him working hard on the immediate patent survey for the Empire Zinc Company and that there is much patent work that is taking up much of his time. The new work is to be right there in Kelly and it is not in rough terrain where large timbers will not get in the way as has been the fact in previous projects. The second half of the letter is about horses such as "Blue" to be given additional grain to get him in good order to sell. He thinks that "Billy" and "Nellie" should also be fattened up to make them more salable. Lastly, Will complaints that his instrument, his transit, is not reliable at the moment and he is having to use the solar techniques in the morning which is the most dependable. He is making sure that all his previous corners are correct. He closes with "Good bye, Will."

Walter Starr, Jean sister Jessie's son dated August 22, from Mount Vernon, Ohio:

Dear Uncle Will:

You have certainly made us a tempting offer and we both appreciated even if we can't accept. There are several reasons why I don't think I would better go out again now.

Ned, Helen and Jean are all going to school. Mabel has a school away. This would leave Mildred to keep up the house or houses. Next I can't make up my mind whether I want to go out to New Mexico to stay and last, I am looking into small manufacturing business here that I may go into. I will tell you more about it later on if it turns to anything.

Ned hasn't quite decided what to do but I think maybe he will go. He says he hates to make the long trip alone and wants to know if you want any more help.

He has got a job that he cannot leave for two or three weeks.

We will write more definitely later.

Hope you are all well, I am.

Yours sincerely, Walter

Will's letter dated October 21, 1907, in Kelly, New Mexico is to Jean and is on Will's U. S. Deputy Mineral Surveyor letterhead. His working with Ned, trying to finish up the work in Kelly and as soon as that is done they will be going up on the" Stonewall Group." He hopes it will only take two days but they are thoroughly sick of the rain for it has steadily rained for the last week or better. They're going to a moving picture show tonight, "so we are all interested." It is to show in Kelly tonight, Magdalena tomorrow and Socorro the following evening. He suggests that they go.

"Kelly is very interesting, studying the geology. I'm trying very hard to pick up some geology and I believe I am getting on to it some. I will learn quite a good deal when we do the work for Mr. Brown and Water Canyon."

Will comments that their friend, Kenneth Lindsay, was looking to come out if there is work would probably be able to help, but he hopes that Ned will be a reliable assistant. He closes with "we went out without a lunch today expecting to get back by noon but did not get through till four and we were pretty weak and hungry I can tell you. Good by, Will." He adds a postscript that the movie was pretty good last night; the circus parade animal shows trained animals and all.

A letter dated January 12, 1908, was to me one the most interesting finds of all the letters that I have. My grandmother showed me this letter at least 40 years ago or more. I have been interested in renewable energy and self sustaining living ideas as far back as I can remember. As he opens in this letter, Will is inquiring into an article about solar powered engines with the thought of maybe incorporating this type of power into irrigation systems.

```
                                                    Jan. 12, 1908.
Mr. Frank Shuman,
     Tacony, Pa.
Dear sir;-
          I was much interested in reading the article in the Technical
World, some time ago describing your Solar Engine.
   A large part of my time and professional work is for the developement
of the water resources of this part of New Mexico. There are large tracts
of very desireable land here which would be available if a sufficiently
cheap system of pumping could be found. It would seem as if your engine
would solve the problem.
   Doubtless when you have made tests of your apparatus on sufficiently
large scale, and under sufficiently variouf conditions, you will establish
agencys, or have the plants established under royalties in different parts
of the country.  It occured to me that in connection with my profession
as engineer I might be able to accomplish good results in the introduction
of the plants to this part of the country, and if I were given the exclusive
controll of large enough territory so that I could give most of my time to
the business I think a great deal could be done.
   In years past I have had a good deal of the practical mechanical experiance
needed in the erection of the plants, so that I would be competent to see that
the mechanics I would associate myself with were doing thier work right.
When you are ready put the apparatus into general use I would be glad to
consider taking the controll of some territory.
                    Yours very truly,
```

Walter Starr, Will and Jean's nephew writes from Mount Vernon, February 24, 1908:

Dear Uncle Will,

I'm sitting at the south window and the sun is scolding hot although the ground is covered with snow and thermometer is 30° below zero.

Frank Blue and Cecil Brenthinger were up here yesterday. Frank says he's going out to New Mexico to help you and he will wanted to know something about the country, what he would need on the trip etc. Frank said you did not have your party made up yet and Cecil Brenthinger wants to go out just for the trip. He has been working in Arnold's bookstore for four or five years, he is almost Ned's age I guess and is a good straight fellow. I think you will like him personally better than Frank Blue and I think he will be as good or better worker. He's about my build and a good walker. Ned can tell you about him. He has no interaction of staying out there but just intends to take a vacation and get some experience.

Well I would be delighted to go out on another trip like the one we took two years ago, but guess I can't now, and Ned never said what the job was but I got the idea somewhere that it was the Texas line job to my right,

I must stop now as it is time to go to work. We are all well and hope you are the same. Remember me to Ned, Kenneth and the rest of the family.

Goodbye, Walter

March 31 finds Jean in Mount Vernon and Will in Socorro acknowledging that Will is starting a project in Clayton, New Mexico. Jean half expects him to come to Mount Vernon after the Clayton project is complete.

Family out for a drive in a large wagon and matched horse team.
Will is the one driving and Marjorie is the one horse.

March 29, Will types a great letter to Jean, being at home and allows him to use the typewriter.

WILLIAM H. HERRICK
U. S. DEPUTY MINERAL SURVEYOR

Socorro, New Mexico, March 29, 1908.

Dear Jean;-

It is about dark and I have just finished the milking and feeding and I can write a few minutes till supper is ready.
I got your first letter after getting home this morning, and also one from Dietzgen saying that the instrument would be shipped tomorrow, and one from Mr. Lott explaining that he did not have time to call me when in Albuquerque but would be ready to take the matter up sometime in the future. It is not likley that we can get away before Wednsday or Thursday. Mr Bursom told me yesterday that he had been given power to make sale of the city lands and he said he would call the trade made and there was no doubt that the council would ratify the trade for the land below town. I happened to be near the land as he was driving to San Antonio and I rode along to the land and showed him the lines.
We had the church meeting today but I will tell about that later as I must stop now.
Here it is Monday night and I have just got time to finish this letter. Well about the meeting. I got to thinking that it was a shame for the two families to run a delay proceedings over the heads of the majority of the church without there knowing what was going on, or the results. Mr. Twining and I had some talk and he thought it was not right to let the matter slide entirely. I had talked to Mr. Meeker a time or two and he understood what was being done, and he understood why we had not felt like interfering, in fact we talked the whole matter over and he decided to go, though he did say that he thought that only those two families were the only ones against him. So I went to Mrs. Cook Friday and asked her what she thought about the matter. She thought we ought not to let Mr. Meeker go, or at least people should have a chance to say whether they wanted him or not.

I told her that we had talked it over and decided that since we were to be away during the hard part of the season and could not help we could not take any stand now. but if she would talk to the ladies who were to be here and if they were willing to stand by him they ought to have a chance to say if they wanted him. There were several at the congregational meeting and the pastoral commitee read a letter from Mr. Gass which said that the two churches could not be united and that this church would be expected to raise a large part of the money, or have this charge united with some other one. If however the church had a man to themselves the Board would give perhaps $200. Miss Fitch moved that the commitee be continued, but no one seconed the motion. Mrs Bear said she would like to have the church vote as to whether they wanted Mr. Meeker or not. Mr. Twining made such a motion, Mrs Cook seconed. The ballot was 10 for and 3 against. Mr. Terry said several times that we ought to see what we could do about salary before we call him, and thought the money could not be raised for him. Nothing was done, however about salary, and I felt badly but maybe it is as well for when we told Mr. Meeker he said Dr. Gass had offered to come and raise the money. Mr. Twining and I are to meet Dr. Gass tomorrow morning as he passes through to Magdalena and ask him to arrange to do that. Mr. M. will stay if he finds the sentement is generally for him, and will go if it seems to be against him. So you see we are still in the midst of intrigues and counter plots.

I must go down to the hotel to mail this now. The boys are down from Kelly over Sunday, and they will stay till we go away I think. The cow is fresh and I fear I will not be able to sell her. I sold her to Mr. Avery but backed out because I could not discount the note he was to give. The man from San Antonio came to look at her and when she charged at his little boys he backed out. I will let Lee Hoffman have her for her keep if I find no buyer soon Good night dearset,

—Will.

On the same day Jean writes from Mount Vernon wondering when and if he will be coming home soon. She is anxious to hear about his meeting in Albuquerque with some men that had been planned. She hopes that they will get around to the work and that Will will be able to take on the job. It is an eight page letter which she continues about the fact that she is lonely despite all the people that come into her life. "Poor little Sarah" has been very sick to the point that she has been in bed even through Jean's mother's birthday. She had to carry Sarah down the stairs to be able to be a part of the 83 candles birthday cake.

Other members of the family are in school and thinks that she is going to take hold of the work all right. Jean goes to Chicago on a shopping trip to buy clothes for the girls and she talks about a couple of presents for other people. Charles has mentioned to her that he knows a hearing specialist from the university in hearing and had hopes that Will will stop and see him when he comes through Chicago for whatever treatment might be a available. It's late and time for bed and Jean closes with "good night sweet dearest."

The month of April, 1908, Jean has the kids in Mount Vernon and Will is working hard on the Clayton project, while Jean is expecting to receive the project notes on the Fort Bayard job. Business seems to be quite good for a change. Jean's letter of April 2th is much like most of her recent letters, semi-upbeat, little down, lonely, worried about money, all the common problems of married life and raising children.

Mt. Vernon Ohio
April 2, 1908

Dear Will:—

I have been looking for another letter from you and think it will come tomorrow morning unless you were too much hurried with getting off on your trip to write me for I think you must surely be started by this time. If not I hope you have been having some work to do or you would be very restless and lonesome. I happened to think yesterday in the money question that the dividend check would be coming soon and was much relieved. Also Willie astonished me by telling me we have $72.00 in the Building and loan. So it

2

teresting; Jean is so fine looking and Helen is so cute the giggly.

Sarah has been having a bad sty on her eye. I dont believe I told you that Cosart said he could not find anything wrong with her heart, her sick spell did not appear to be from it — just a dreadful state of the stomach and some fever. I got Sarah a coat today and it was a good day for it for it was so cold she complained she was nearly frozen and I thot it a good time to look for a winter coat and got a fleece coat for $3.48

Friday morning. Ther. down to 24° this morning.

Sunday. Here my letter is unfinished yet. When your letter came saying you would get away Wed. or Thurs. I did not know as it

that fire? We did not know
it did you? I felt worried
over the money for I knew
I ought to "or" having money
for every expenses" these days
and combined with Essie as we
did before if we stay here or
as long as we stay here. Charlie's
have gone out into the country
and Florence & Helen and Jean
came home at 6:45 last night
from Oberlin. I wish they were in
here so I could see more of them,
I mean Charlie & Docie, tho I will
enjoy going out there when it warms
up; it is colder today than any
winter we have had in A. M. I think
Beulah & I went to prayer meeting with
Jessie, Millie & Helen tis evening for
Mother felt so chilly that she dread
to go out and I thot rather to go
with the rest than to go to our own
alone. Jean and Helen are so in

was of any use to hurry off my letter as I suppose you will not get it until you reach Clayton now anyway unless you should be detained about getting off and I trust you will not have much more delay. They had a wonderful day in the Pres. church to-day or in all the churches I suppose. 71 joined the Pres. church to-day and 56 the Congregationalist and I heard 284 were to join the Methodist 30 the Episcopal. I did not hear about any of the other churches but I presume some from the Grah Tabernacle meetings probably went to every church in town. There is a movement on foot for organizing a Y.W.C.A. here too. I was

Hughes from Cincinnati is here working it up and as I am always interested in her work Mildred and I went to the meeting this P.M. Miss Hughes is a very good speaker. I sort of wish Frank Blue would come around to see me before he starts for New Mexico but I suppose he is not likely to do so; they live in Gambier and his people telephoned to me but he won't be worked up over the trip as much as the people were over when he should go I presume. It has been raining all day to-day — not very hard most of the time not drizzling and the grass is getting lovely and green — it was pretty gray when we came, then just started to get green but now is growing lovely. I must write to Ida now

For Mother,

Monday - a card from Ned with picture of the fire tells me that you did not get off before Brentinger was to get there and that the instrument was not there. I fear you are worried. I do not understand whether that means the solar compass from Dietzgen or the new inst. from Gurley or both. I think maybe I better send this letter to Socorro again. I am sorry I did not send it before this time now. I suppose it will be all right for me to direct to Clayton after this as I suppose there is no doubt but that will be your P.O. but I fancy you will say something about that when you actually get ready to start. I can hardly imagine how you have kept occupied all this time since I came away and you have no one to waste your time on.

   Good by Dearest
     Jean.

I am a little afraid you have forgotten to send me the Manual and paper have you not? If so I presume Ned can send them or Miss Reid.

for mother,

Monday - a card from Ned with picture of the fire tells me that you did not get off before Brentinger was to get there and that the instrument was not there. I fear you are worried. I do not understand whether that means the solar compass from Dietzgen or the new inst. from Gurley or both. I think maybe I better send this letter to Socorro again. I am sorry I did not send it before this time now. I suppose it will be all right for me to direct to Clayton after this as I suppose there is no doubt but that will be your P.O. but I fancy you will say something about that when you actually get ready to start. I can hardly imagine how you have kept occupied all this time since I came away and you have no one to waste your time on.

Good by Dearest
Jean.

I am a little afraid you have forgotten to send me the Manual and paper have you not? If so I presume Ned can send them or Miss Reid.

177

William is in Lamy, New Mexico, April 7, just passing through on the train. As you will read, Will has to spend a lot of time with horses and wagons and such. Boy can I empathize with the work that it takes being a horseman myself.

WILLIAM H. HERRICK
U. S. DEPUTY MINERAL SURVEYOR

Lamy, ~~Socorro~~, New Mexico, April 7, 1908

Dear Jean:—

We reached Albuquerque last evening and got a few supplies. I rode out about a mile with the boys and found a deserted house where I changed my clothes and sent the boys on for about one hour's more drive while I walked back and stayed over night at the hotel. I intended to go into camp with them, but it was so early that I decided to let them go on. The trip has gone on very well, so far. We made the trip to Albuquerque in about 3 days. I missed the train I should have taken this morning so I have to wait here at ~~Lamy~~ all day from noon to 6 tonight. I think I can do all I want to tomorrow and get here Thurs. noon, that will be the time I look for them here. It will not matter much if I should be delayed and not get here till evening as the horses will be pretty tired. I will be glad to get out of this much of the trip. The driving is hard work. The 4 horses to the big wagon is a great help, but it is a job to drive them together. It has become very windy since noon and the boys will have another bad day. Saturday was a regular sandstorm all day but Sunday and Monday were very pleasant.

If I can sell horses and wagons when we are through the work we will all come back by train. I would hate to give up Nan, but since we will still have Kate and all her colts maybe that will be enough horses to winter again.

There is not much to write now and I don't feel very ambitious waiting here at the station.

I tellphoned to Prof. Zight last night and as he was comming to town for something he called on me at the hotel for a few minutes. We talked a little about plans for reclaiming river bottom land, but didn't have much time.

Last night there was quite a contest between the republicans and Democrats over the election which is to be today. There were big bonfires and speechs on the street. I would like to know how they come out. Did I tell you that Smileys have two children sick now? Mrs Hills little girl was getting on very well last I heard, but school will not open again now for some time I fear. You never have said much about Sarah or what Robert said about her, whether there is any heart trouble or not. Dr Furgeson wanted you to ask Robert to write him about the case.

I have three hours yet to wait, but I am getting so sleepy I will finish this up and see if I cant sleep a little here.

good by Will

A letter from the Superintendent of Public Schools, Socorro, New Mexico, Mr. R. W. Twinning is addressed to Will and is trying to search him down in Clayton on behalf of the church to ask if he can aid the church with a financial pledge because they are looking for a new pastor. Dated April 18, 1908:

Office Of Superintendent Of Public Schools
R. W. Twining, Superintendent

Socorro, New Mexico, Apr. 18, 1908

Mr. W. H. Herrick
    Clayton, N. Mex.
Dear Mr. Herrick:-

  I don't know your whereabouts; but suppose you are in Clayton or will be by the time this reaches there. Hope you have had a good journey.

  Mr. Gass has been down here; he had a call meeting of the trustees last Thur. night. They appointed Mrs. Geo Cook and myself as a committee to raise the subscription for pastor. I had already told Mr. Gass that I did not want to take up that work; but they went ahead all the same. Mrs Cook refuses to take any part in the matter; so it looks as though the burden would fall on someone else. The prospect for a good subscription is very encouraging; nearly everyone is gladly renewing and many are doubling what they have been doing.

  Some of the doubtful subscriptions have been cheerfully renewed.

Office Of Superintendent Of Public Schools
R. W. Twining, Superintendent

Socorro, New Mexico,_____190__

it offers a much better salary, also a better chance for advancing in school work.

Mr. Hammond is a member of the Baptist church there and I judge a very nice man

I would like to know what you think about the town there and the surrounding country; so you can write anything you wish and say what you wish there.

I don't know but it will be wise for me to be thankful to get the school there and not be too particular. I have been corresponding with a good school in Western Kansas; but am most afraid to risk that climate yet.

I hope you will have a pleasant stay in Union Co. and get along nicely with your work. Will be glad to hear from you any time.

With kind regards

R. W. Twining

Will sends Jean a great letter, full of optimism and seems to be happy with the job and the environment. The letter is on the Hotel Bruns, Clayton, New Mexico letterhead and is dated April 18, 1908.

HOTEL BRUNS
CLAYTON, NEW MEXICO

April 18, 1908

Dear Jean:-

We reached here last night in good condition. The transit was here held by a $2.65 C.O.D. I hustled around and got it started to Santa Fe last night. I had only half hour to get identified and get it off last night. We will have to wait now till that gets back. About Wednesday I suspect. In the mean time we have established a camp just on the edge of town and Monday Kenneth and I will take an exploring trip to the South. I will be able to report the conditions found on the line and maybe get a larger appropriation for the survey if needed.

I have been busy today getting located, wagon repaired and supplies

HOTEL BRUNS
CLAYTON, NEW MEXICO

bought. $40 worth the first order and that mostly for a few days stay, but it includes 3 cases of canned goods and a bed for Ed New.
We had a pretty good trip 360 miles. Saw very fine land about Las Vegas and from there here is all good land and roads were good. We made 30 miles and more a day. Left R.R. at Wagon Mound. Saw a good many settlers about that place and began to see them 15 miles before we reached Clayton. All land near town is taken, and there are said to be settlers all up and down the State line. I had a letter from Mr. Lott asking if I wanted to become a director in the Company which is to develope the Antonio Sedillo Grant.

HOTEL BRUNS
CLAYTON, NEW MEXICO

I was so long in getting his letter that my acceptance may be too late. He said that $20 000 was set aside for subdivision of the land and $200 000 for irrigation project.
I will mail this now and get things settled at camp. I will give up my room here today. I probably can write more tomorrow.

Yours
Will.

There are three letters, April 20, from Edward Starr to Will, April 22 and 23rd from Will to Jean. Edward was a nephew of theirs and his is in Kelly and is helping Will with various projects. Jean's letters are again about the progress of the surveying project near Clayton, New Mexico.

April 24, 1908, Will receives a letter that he has been waiting for. It confirms that the work done on the Fort Bayard Military Reservation.

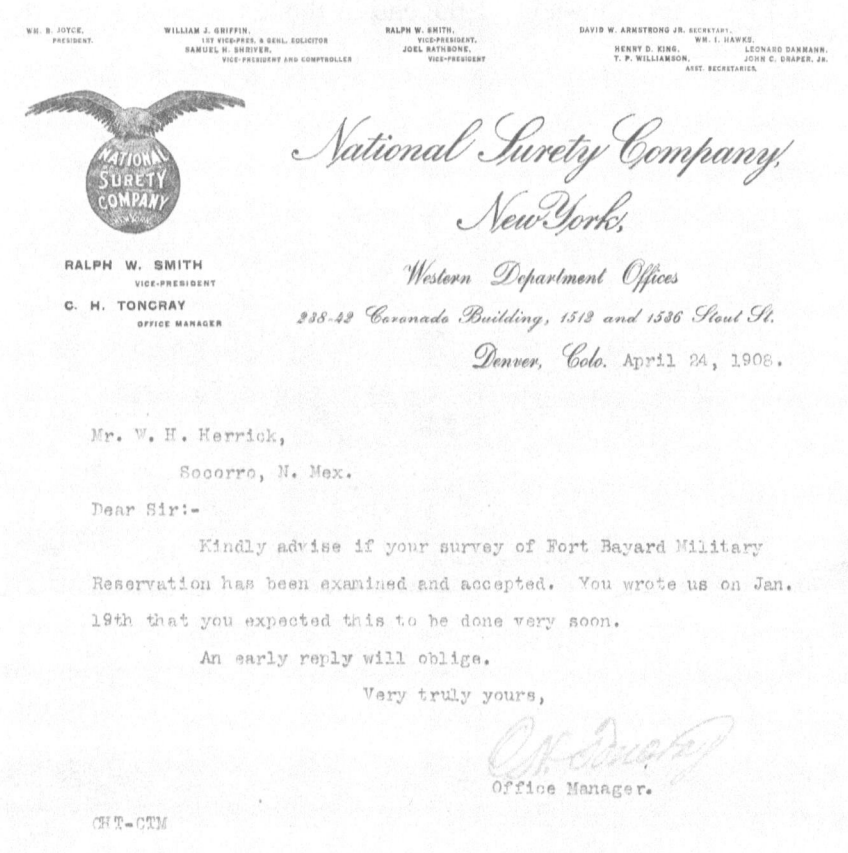

Jean's letter of May 4 has to do with the weather, the cold, the rain, all things that happen in the spring, both in Ohio where she is and North East New Mexico, where Will is. She has gained four pounds which is great, "I think likely I have gained it since I came here, eating and sleeping so much." She understands that their nephew Edward is now the camp cook.

As usual, with the other major concern of their life, money is another part of the letter; she has recently been in Chicago and saw Charlie, who commented had he had an extra hundred dollars. He would not have mentioned it but for the fact that he knew that the government money was to arrive, but the problem as usual, was when it would arrive. Her love and loneliness shows up at the end of the letter, hoping that they will be together soon.

There's a great letter from Will and Jean's nephew Edward:

WILLIAM H. HERRICK
U. S. Deputy Mineral Surveyor

Kelly, ~~Socorro~~ New Mexico. May 4th, 1908.

Mr W. H. Herrick.
  Clayton,
    New Mexico.
      Dear Uncle;—
                  As it is snowing outside and we have our platting and figuring pretty well up, I think I will write you a report of our work this morning.

So far we have located all the corners on the ground except eight. All traverses have been brought within limits except the one closing on your S.E. Stonewall corner. This is off 14 ft. in latitude and 7.58 ft in departure in a traverse of 7000. The tie which you accepted from Smiths survey is not on the map; will I find the copy of your field notes for Stonewall Group at the house? I do not know what can be the matter with the above traverse, but have not thoroughly investigated it yet.

About the limit of error, one foot in a thousand seems large, when compared with the limit for public land which is 25 links in four miles or about 4/5 of a foot in a thousand. I supposed the greater error would be allowed in the case of public land surveys. ~~Perhaps~~ I am wrong about one or the other limits of error and as I do not find it given in the manual, I wish you would assure me about the limit for Mineral Surveying. What do you think about trying to make traverses close closer than the limit of error it after first trial. I suppose a certain amount of retracing is a good thing.

I have made no topography notes so far nor have I kept account of the magnetic variation. Can they be supplied closely enough, the one from memory and the other the same for all lines.

The manual speaks of material errors in previous surveys, do you think that refers to the size of the are error or does it mean any error that effects the length or course of a line?

I have found in lines, I believe that checked closer than two minutes, and some of them had well established corners with crosses in them.

Well I guess thats all I have to say about the work. Mr Brown has been in Arizona for 10 days, is probably back now, hasn't been here since we first came up.

Katy and the colt are doing well.

Good Bye

Edward N. Starr

P.S. Have looked again for the limit of error in the manual and find it to be only .5 ft. instead of 1.0 foot in 1000.0. Well that seems more like it and I guess anybody ought to be satisfied if things close that close.

Jean's letter of May 20, 1908 and then Will's letter of May 22 are quite interesting in the fact that they each write letters of similar content and yet neither one has seen the other's letter. Basically, the Clayton project is becoming strictly tiresome, it's taking too long and they probably will not break even on the money part of the job.

A.B. Fitch sends this letter dated May 24, 1908, thus adding to the complexity of their lives:

A. B. FITCH
CIVIL AND MINING ENGINEER
HOLLYWOOD, CALIFORNIA

MAX B. FITCH
MINING ENGINEER
EL PASO, TEXAS

HOMESTEAD DEVELOPMENT COMPANY

El Paso, Texas.
May 24th 1908.

Mr. W. H. Herrick,
   Socorro, N. Mex.,

Dear Sir:-

      We have decided to either sell or rent our home here and move back to Socorro. I may be able to accomplish this within thirty days and may not be able to do it until this Fall or Winter.

      I wanted to write you about it now so that you can be on the lookout for some other place, but it will not be necessary for you to move until you get further notice from me and I will give you as long a time after that as I can.

      I was in Socorro the other day and was very much pleased with the care that you and Mrs. Herrick have given the property.

                 Very truly,

                        Max B. Fitch

Copy sent to you at Clayton, N. Mex..

Up until this time they have been living in the Hilton family house, which is owned by Max at this time.

Will's letter from Clayton of May 26, tells Jean of Max Fitch's plan to move back to Socorro and this is the first mention of building their own house:

> WILLIAM H. HERRICK
> U. S. DEPUTY MINERAL SURVEYOR
>
> Clayton
> SOCORRO, NEW MEXICO May 26, 1908
>
> Dear Jean:-
> We are back in Clayton and through with the body of the work. The question is now whether to disband or no. I have not received the instructions about the southern No. yet. Telegraphed today. I do not know as that will hasten matters as the Santa Fe people are only waiting for word from Washington I suppose. I still have several corners to finish and some to change on south and will make a short trip down there anyway. I think I will let them all go but Charlie and Ed. Now tomorrow possibly, anyway if Kenneth decides he and Edger want to go now.
> We finished before noon today. It was very windy when we got to town 2130 and I did not clean up at all but tried to sell horses. Thought I had Molly sold but the man backed out after we had tried her driving single. She went all right but I guess the man was a little afraid she was not gentle enough for him. The wind quieted down after sun down and at dark I went on the street to get some toilet soap. saw most of the boys there and treated them to ice cream and came back to camp built a little fire to warm some water to

and took a bath here or some vacant lots in
town. I am now in bed writing with the lantern
set on a box at the head of the bed.
The wind tore most of of our tent up. We have
not tried to put up a tent for some time.
I got a letter from Max Fitch today saying
that they were coming back to Socorro as
soon as they can rent their house in El Paso.
Might be in 30 days and might not be till
fall, but would try to give us plenty of time.
I will write him tomorrow that we will move
soon. I think I will move when I get down.
I suppose we better take Alice's house for a while
till we can get one of our own perhaps. What
do you say. Maybe I better write to Alice now.
The Zimmermans are going away in a week or so.
I guess the rent would be the same in either
house so if Max Fitch will say we can keep the
house through July maybe that would be best.
Maybe I will ask him if he can do that.
This is a strained position to write so I will close
though I am not sleepy.
I will write again as soon as I know what
is to be done about the work here.
                                Good night Will
Wed. Morning. No mail yet. I think I will disband the
party. Keeping Ed Nus and Charlie till I get through. If I find
there is more work I can hire another man down there.

Jean's letter of May 27, is almost a copy of Wills May 26 letter because she has received a forwarded letter earlier. She has had to move the family to the upstairs of Uncle Charles house but it should work out.

I have three letters written in the month of June from Jean though I know Will has been writing more than one letter because she mentions other letters in hers." Mount Vernon, Ohio, June 1, 1908, my dearest, I have hardly been able to keep calm since the mail at noon brought me your letter saying you would soon be starting first for Socorro and then soon be starting here." The summers good, the kids are fine and she and all the family are planning some nice time that will hopefully give Will some time to rest. The 15th of June will be their anniversary, their 14th.

Guess what. The June 7th letter from Jean, is basically a carbon copy of the June 1 letter that finds friends visiting with the family looking forward to his getting home but realizes at this point he may not make it on time. In the letter on the 10th, I feel Jean's attitude changing just in her opening of the letter: "Your letter with the handbook of field notes came at noon today and I will 'fall to' on the notes tomorrow morning. I looked at them some today but had made arrangements to go out this p.m. I am powerful sleepy tonight but wanted to write you a little note anyway for I want you to get a letter on before the 15th if you cannot come home."

Will's letter of June 5th, which was sent from Socorro, probably didn't arrive in Mount Vernon after all the other letters from Jean had arrived in Socorro. He is sending work to Jean because he feels a bit more consistent in the final typing than if he tried to do it but he still is working on some "Polaris observations" that might help with the final survey of claims in Water Canyon. He fears he will not be home by the 15th on the account of the fact that he needs to be in Magdalena and then on to Kelly and the timing of things just won't allow him to leave to be home on the 15th, their wedding anniversary.

For the year of 1909, I don't have any letters from anybody other than one correspondence between William and his former partner J.T. Park. The former Park, Colville and Herrick Company of Mount Vernon, Ohio, is now the Metropolis Bending Company of Metropolis, Illinois. The five typed pages of the letter starts with how well the bending business is doing even after a year of panic. I guess 1909 was not such a good year in the manufacturing sector of the US economy, for 1906 and 1907 were better but still they are satisfied. He then goes on to describe the well drilling information he has in regard to down driven wells; this is something easily done in places where the water is more than 20 to 25 feet deep and where there is abundance of clean sand and gravel. He describes another process of using an auger where two men can drill down 40 to 50 feet in a day, if there are no rocks. Then J.T. continues on about a sawmill proposition but again without being in New Mexico no one can't really know if it would be cost effective to go into that business and if it were ordinary land and if there was good size soft lumber, as in the East. Wood can be cut at $25 per million (board feet) but it is much shorter distance and probably easier hauling than it is in the West, because of the distances and everything related. Will is always looking into business idea that could make life easier for him and Jean.

A steam powered drilling rig around the turn of the 1900s.

4

THE SCOTS ARRIVE IN THE NEW WORLD -- NEW MEXICO IS THE FIRST STOP

Hugh Chapman Fraser, my Grandfather, was born April 1, 1895, Denny Street, Inverness, Scotland. His father, Hugh Fraser, was the office manager for the Rose Street Foundry Engineering Company Limited, Inverness, Scotland. (See a copy of the Foundry Invoice). He was showing important visitors around the showroom when a stove fell and a sharp point of metal struck him, tearing his trousers making a gash in his thigh. At first he gave the wound little thought but it became infected. Over the next two or more years he went to doctors in Aberdeen, Edinburgh and later to the famous Dr. Joseph Lister, in London. The infection was so advanced that Dr. Lister amputated the leg but it was too late to save his life. Hugh died in 1896 leaving a wife and four children. My great Grandmother Margaret Cameron Fraser, took the four children to live with her mother on the farm in Stratherick, Gorthlick, a valley about 20 miles SE of Inverness.

The photograph is of Hugh and Margaret Fraser early in their married life, maybe a wedding photo. They were married on October 9, 1888, in Inverness, Scotland.

Hugh's earliest known photograph in America, maybe from his entry papers. ca. 1916, age 21.

Folio _____

Rose Street Foundry,
Inverness _____ 189

To _____
The Rose Street Foundry & Engineering
Company Limited.
IRONFOUNDERS, ENGINEERS, MILLWRIGHTS AND
189 _____ IRON MERCHANTS.

£   s   d

To Amount of Account Rendered.

The Invoice from "The Rose Street Foundry & Engineering Company Limited," Scotland, ca. 189_s.
This is where Hugh and his father worked.

The Fraser Family, Daisy, Anna, Hugh, Grandmother Cameron, with Margaret (Mother) seated and Jack standing and holding her arm. 1898.

Here is how my mother, Jean Cameron Fraser Spiller and I combined to write the early story of my Grandfather's life:

In 1905 John (Jack) Duncan, Hugh's brother, who was five years older went to Magdalena, New Mexico, to live with Aunt Bessie (Mrs. J.S. Mactavish). Mr. Mactavish promised to see that Jack was educated and had a job. Mr. Mactavish was in the mercantile business associated with the Becker Companies in Belen, Magdalena and Springerville, Arizona. Jack went back to Scotland for a visit in 1910 or 1911 and when he returned to Magdalena, Ann Elizabeth (Anna), the oldest sister was 18 years old, came with him.

Hugh started school in September 1901 and continued till he was fifteen, the age the law requires children attend school. About this time Mrs. Fraser, Margaret Catherine (Daisy), the youngest sister and Hugh moved back to Inverness.

Hugh now went to work. He said that during the summer, he and other children picked strawberries (which he did not like) for a cranky framer and they had to whistle while they picked the strawberries, that way they couldn't be eating them. His first real job was with Macrae & Dick, Inverness's newly expanding livery and now automobile company. This is where he learned to drive a car. One of his first assignments was in County Caithness in Northern Scotland. In April of 1912 he drove a mail truck on the Isle of Skye. Macrae and Dick then sent him to the hunting lodge of the Ismay family, owners of the White Star Steamship Line. He drove a car to a hotel where he met guests. His predecessor had run off the road into a lake and his passenger drowned and when he saw the fate of the passenger and car, jumped in the lake and drowned himself.

That is how my grandfather got the job as chauffeur for the summer. After the summer season he went back to Inverness and was an apprentice in the auto repair department at the Rose Street Foundry, the same place where his father had worked.

Anna, Jack, mother Margaret, Hugh and Daisy in Inverness at their cousin's Photography Studio before Jack and Anna leave home for the Americas, 1911.

Hugh, his mother and Daisy after Jack and Anna are in New Mexico, 1915.

Departure of a Shinty Player

PRESENTATION FROM FELLOW-WORKMEN

Mr Hugh Fraser.

Above we reproduce a photograph of Mr Hugh Fraser, who was in the employment of the Rose Street Foundry, in their garage at Shore Street, for some time past. He was also a playing member of the Clachnacuddin Shinty Club. Before leaving town he was met by a number of friends and fellow-workmen in the Commercial Hotel and made the recipient of a handsome hunting lever watch, suitably inscribed. Mr A. Irvine, the manager of the Works, occupied the chair, and referred to Mr Fraser's capabilities as a workman and a friend. After the usual toasts, Mr Fraser feelingly replied. The remainder of the evening was spent in song and sentiment. Mr Fraser left for Mexico last week, with the best wishes of a large circle of friends.

The clip from the Highland Times, Thursday, May 28, 1914. My grandfather, Hugh has left for "Mexico," hopefully no one will go looking for him there.

Hugh's Driver's License for a Motor Car or Motor Cycle the day before he leaves for New Mexico.

Hugh C. Fraser and friend ready for war. They did their Basic Training at Fort Bliss, Texas. This picture is El Paso as they wait for the train that will take them off to Europe.

By 1914 Great Britain was already involved in World War 1 and by 1916 Hugh's mother was afraid he would be called into the British Army. In addition to his brother and sister Anna already living in New Mexico, at least three of his mother's relatives were also living here. Hugh, Daisy and their mother entered the US through the port in Philadelphia in the spring of 1916. From there they took the train through the new America to end up in Reserve, New Mexico. Jack Fraser had taken over the old Reserve Mercantile and was established there. Jack had married Ola McCarty from a local Reserve family. Their family grows with Margaret (Peggy) born in 1917 in Reserve.

World War 1 was the opportune time for Hugh to become a Citizen of the United States by joining the US Army as a volunteer. You were made a Citizen by enlisting in the military. I am not certain that Hugh's Mother knows anything about the enlistment. This is one of the reasons that they left Scotland, to keep Hugh from being drafted into the British Army, now he goes and joins the American Army.

Hugh, Daisy and Mrs. Margaret Fraser move to Magdalena, New Mexico, where Margaret will live until her death in 1933. Most of the New Mexico Fraser's are buried in Magdalena.

Hugh was stationed near Paris, France when the war ended. Both photos show Sergeant Fraser and his compatriots on duty at a Prisoner of War Camp. That is a "Gas Mask" around their necks.

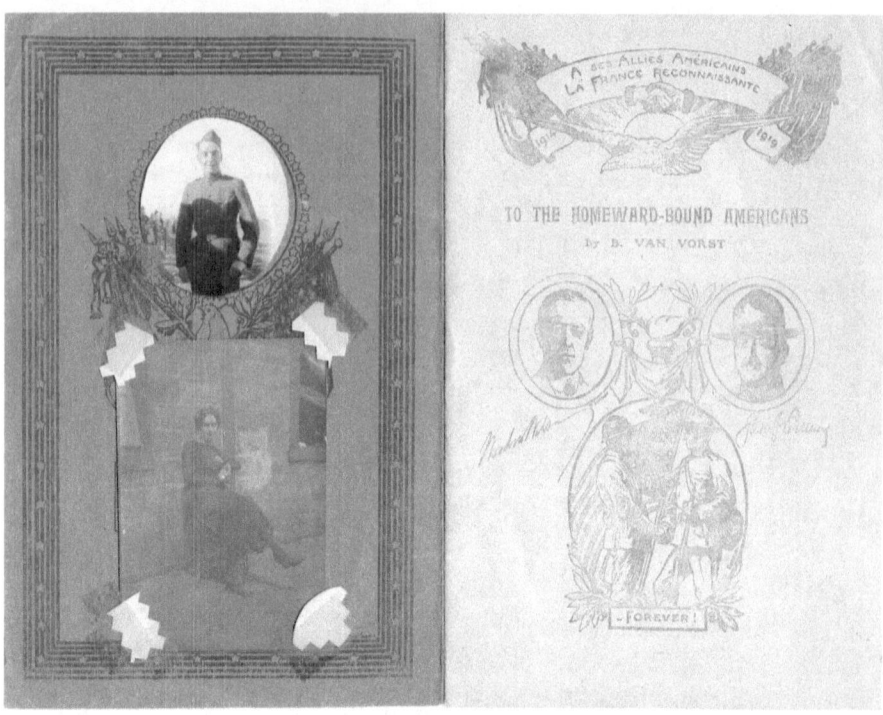

The opening pages of what was given to the American Soldiers as they were to leave France. Hugh is the small photo left top, his girl friend at the time is the photo below his, but her name is unknown.

Hugh writes his sister Daisy but the stamp and postmarks are missing due to time and miles.

ON ACTIVE SERVICE
WITH THE
AMERICAN EXPEDITIONARY FORCES

Nov. 13th 1918

Dear Anna,

    Glad to get your letter and to hear you keep well and like your work.

    Since I wrote last so much has happened that it is hard to realize how important the events have been and it all came so suddenly that we could hardly believe it was true.

    On the day before yesterday about eleven o'clock in the fore-noon we got official notice that the armistice had been signed and every ship in the harbor all the locomotives and factories started their steam-whistles blowing and for half an hour you would have thought

This letter is from my Grandfather in France to his sister Anna in New Mexico two days after the Armistice of World War 1 on the 11th Month on the 11th Day on the 11th Hour. The letter is censored and okayed by a S.E. Johnson, Capt. USMC.

2/
Hades was let loose. For the rest of the day work was out of the question, and most of us got off and proceeded at once to town to take in the celebrations. You can imagine how the French people felt who had waited for this day for more than four years and who had had so many disappointments.

    For an incredibly short time the town was covered with flags of France and the Allies and a number of bands were parading the main streets and the boulevards, and people gathered from miles around so it was practically impossible to pass through the crowds.

    It was a great day for France and for a while the lid was off, although to some it recalled sad memories and many a tear was shed, for this part of the country has given

3/

many a young man to the cause.

However, France is having her revenge for the blow she had in 1871 and she doesn't think any price too great to pay for it. Everyone was saying "How I would like to be back in the States tonight" and I bet you had a day to be remembered.

We are carrying on just the same as ever for it isn't all over yet and there is so much work to be done before we even think of going back home. It is up to us to help out France as much as we can for the reconstruction period is going to be a hard time after all she has lost and suffered.

Anyway, we are all glad that the fighting has ceased and it doesn't seem likely that it will it will be resumed as Germany has had about enough of it along with her internal troubles and won't be in a position to cause any more trouble. It will be a great relief to all you folks back home and the time won't seem so long now.

    Will write soon again so will close now.
        Your Affectionate Brother
          Hugh C. Fraser

    OK
      S. E. Johnson
        Capt USMC

Reserve Looking west across the valley towards Glenwood. It is not a very big town. 1919–1920.

After Hugh's discharge from the Army he visited Inverness, for the last time, before he returned to Reserve, New Mexico. I have heard stories that he worked with Uncle Bill Jones as forest ranger in the Frisco/Gila River area.

I guess there was no limit in those days as there are today. My Grandfather is the one holding the end of the line.

In 1919 he attended New Mexico College of Agriculture and Mechanic Arts, New Mexico State University now, and received a degree from the Auto Mechanics Department in June 1920. His first job after college was in Kelly near Magdalena. He said he was the most important man in town, because he kept the power on for lights and water. In the early 1920s the mines were closing and there was little need for his expertise. He went to Reserve where Jack was successfully running the Reserve Mercantile.

New Mexico College of Agriculture and Mechanic Arts

THIS IS TO CERTIFY THAT

Hugh Chapman Fraser

has completed in a satisfactory manner the course prescribed for the

Auto Mechanics Department

in the above institution

In Testimony Whereof we have affixed our signatures at the College, Mesilla Park, New Mexico, this 14th day of June 1920.

President of the College

HARRY S. NEW

POSTMASTER GENERAL OF THE UNITED STATES OF AMERICA

TO ALL TO WHOM THESE PRESENTS SHALL COME, GREETING:

Know ye, That reposing special trust and confidence in the intelligence, diligence, and discretion of _Hugh Fraser_, I have appointed and do commission him Postmaster at _Reserve_, in the County of _Catron_, State of _New Mexico_, and do authorize and empower him to execute and fulfill the duties of that office according to the laws of the United States and the regulations of the Post Office Department, and to have and to hold the said office, with all the rights and emoluments thereunto legally appertaining, during the pleasure of the Postmaster General of the United States.

IN TESTIMONY WHEREOF I have hereunto set my hand, and caused the seal of the Post Office Department to be affixed, at the city of Washington, this _second_ day of January, in the year of our Lord one thousand nine hundred and twenty-four and of the Independence of the United States of America the one hundred and forty-eighth.

By direction of the Postmaster General.

First Assistant Postmaster General

Postmaster General

Hugh was appointed Postmaster at Reserve, January 2, 1924. The mail arrived from Silver City or Socorro only three times on a good week. He also had a Ford automobile dealership and garage. He didn't have a showroom, just pictures and a few options. When a car sold, my grandfather would have to go to Denver, Colorado and pick up the car for the buyer and drive it back to Reserve.

Reserve is the place that brings the Herrick's and the Fraser's family in contact with each other. Reserve is the County Seat for Caton County where William and Jean Herrick must complete and record land surveys and abstracts so there is the possibility that they came in contact with the Fraser brothers.

These two photographs of the Reserve Mercantile show pre-autos, still horses, mules and wagons. The second photograph shows quite a sizable expansion from the first photograph. Jack Fraser had been in Reserve since at least 1917 when he married Ola Jones.

The Post Office sign is to the far right; my Grandmother is in the doorway with my Grandfather to the right of her. These photos are from the 1920s–1930s.

The Reserve Mercantile now has telegraph poles and lines and has expanded from the first photo. Electricity for the store cooler and lights, as well as both Frasers homes are supplied by their own generator. A new sign and gas pumps have been added in these photos.

Road trip making a pit stop at the Reserve Mercantile.

5

THE AUTO ADDS A NEW ELEMENT TO TRAVEL

A Family picnic made easier by the advent of the auto in everyday life. They could get to their favorite places faster and with more comfort, less effort. Bunny is kneeling in front of the campfire with my grandmother, Sarah, sitting across from her. Great grandmother Jean is standing in the background with one of her older brothers. Miggie is on the far right covering someone and the gentleman in dark clothes, standing, has not been identified.

The automobile's entry into New Mexico, changed life, in that travel times were shortened and a life centered on horses also changed. Family outings now had cars in the photographs.

Pictures of a rodeo from the grandstands; cars and tents are in the distances and the mountains like the mountains around Magdalena. Rodeos were the biggest spectator sport of the time in the West; Baseball was more a big city thing.

Baseball was still a major pastime and there were teams that played the area.

The Herrick women, Sarah, Marjorie, mother Jean and Beulah. Father Will is more than likely the one taking the photograph.

There were no hotels or motels at this time.
Everything had to be packed into and on the cars.
Everyone helped.

The car was used as the high half of the tent and sun shape. This young man must be watching not helping.

There weren't any bridges yet across the sometimes mighty Rio Grande. A flash flood that started many miles away could affect the water levels. There could be quicksand in areas that looked okay but were not.

The dog, Will and Jean sitting are joined by family and friends. The car makes life just a little easier and more people can come along.

On a trip one might not see another soul for days at a time. It would take two plus days to get from Socorro to Reserve, if all went well on the journey.

Jack and Anna Fraser posing in front of the family favorite Ford motor vehicle, Downtown Reserve, 1920s.

The windmill in the distance may be the only sign of human existence other than the road itself and a cow or two. The windmill was also a landmark that could be seen for miles, plus it was a valuable source of much needed water.

Flat tires were the most common problem that occurred on any trip. One had to be able to fix or repair just about any mechanical problem that happened while one was out in the wilderness.

Sometimes the more hands the better.
All the rest could do is stay cool and watch.

The two photos above show that what is set up has to be packed into and onto the car. The lower photo is looking south from the Reserve Mercantile. The automobile really changed life in rural New Mexico that was not serviced by the train.

A car is now parked where once horses would have been standing.

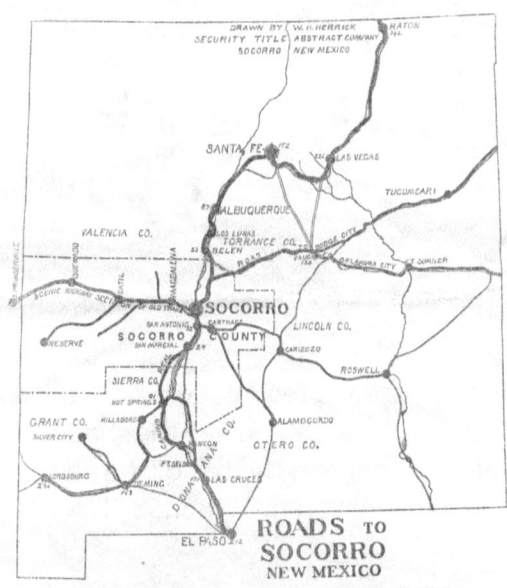

Road map drawn by Will Herrick showing that Socorro was the center of New Mexico.

6

WILL'S DEATH AND THE MARRIAGE OF TWO OF HIS DAUGHTERS

The Herrick ladies are using a technique where there is string is tied to the steadied camera. You can just see the shadow line of the string coming from Marjorie's hand to the left of the photo. The photo is of Marjorie, Jean, Beulah and Sarah, without Will.

May 28, 1920. When one looks into the photograph, one can see two horses pulling a wagon down a flooded Socorro road.

May 29, 1920. This time you can see a man on horseback coming down the flooded road, again in Socorro.

The Christmas season of 1920 started off well with the arrival of Walter Starr, Jean's nephew and his wife Marguerite, daughters Barbara and baby Jessie. Walter was in poor health and the dry weather of Socorro was a great help.

Then while picking Mistletoe, Will falls from a tree breaking his spine and cannot move from his neck to his toes. With no real hospital or medical help available in New Mexico, Jean has Will carefully prepared for a train ride in the baggage car to Chicago and hopefully better help. Jean rides at his side to Chicago while Beulah, who now a student at the University of California, Berkeley, is told to stay at school for now. Marjorie is a senior at the University of Wooster in Ohio and Sarah is a senior in High School in Wooster. They both come home to be with their mother.

In Chicago, Will does not get better and actually turns for the worst. Jean, and by now all the daughters, are in New Mexico in the spring of 1921. It has not been six months but on June 24, 1921, Will dies from starvation as the doctors and the hospital at the University of Chicago where is younger brother C. Judson Herrick was a Professor, have done all they can for him.

William is brought back to New Mexico, his home that he truly loved, and was buried in Socorro. From this time on my grandmother, Sarah (Sam), Beulah (Bunny) and Marjorie (Maggie) all ended up staying with their Mother in Socorro until the first wedding.

Photograph of Bunny and Great Grandmother standing together. This is how I remember my Aunt Bunny and Great-Grandmother, late 1950s.

Marjorie Herrick, the middle daughter, of William and Jean Herrick, marries Charles (Brad) L. Bradbury September 9, 1923. Brad is a student at the New Mexico School of Mines when they met. They are wedded in Socorro but Brad's work will soon take him and his family to Mexico and Bolivia. These two photos are from the wedding day at the Center Street family home in Socorro.

The Bradbury children, Margie, Bill, Emily and Anne (Nancy), on one of their trips to Grandmother Herrick's home in Socorro. Marjorie comes back to New Mexico after Brad dies! My "Aunt Maggie" joins the "Peace Corp" and was in Guatemala from 1963 to 1966 and loved every minute of it.

The gentleman in the top hat is my Great Grandfather, William Spiller. This is a copy of a "Tin Type" photograph, ca. 1850s.

October 2, 1921. A truly Red Letter Day. My father Kenneth Dwight Spiller was born to William E. and Julia Heath Spiller in Dartmouth, Massachusetts. William was a "Millwright" in the mill towns of the East Coast. Julia was a housewife but her father had been a doctor in East Freetown, Massachusetts.

Also in 1921, Sarah gets a job working at the newly-opened bank in Reserve but before the bank is a year old, the bank president is charged with embellishment and the bank closes. Sarah must look for another job so an offer as the new bookkeeper at the Reserve Mercantile Company comes at the right time and this also leads to the romance between my grandparents, Hugh and Sarah.

Hugh leans on the rear fender of the car with his mother Margaret Fraser, in the back seat, outside the Reserve Mercantile.

Mother Jean and Sarah are smiling in front of the camera.
It looks like an Indian woven basket in Jean's hands.
They are together at home in Socorro.

The Living/Music Room in Socorro would never be as bright again.
The Herrick House on Center Street.

The string "selfie" technique used in an earlier photo is used here. Maggie again is pulling the string. This photo is inside the "Bunny Hut" at the base of Socorro Mountain

This is some local color, as retold by my grandmother, Sarah Herrick Fraser:

> In 1921, Reserve was still little changed from the frontier town of earlier times. A railroad was hundreds of miles away, most likely unimproved roads lead out, it was quite isolated.... The only store in town (one of the owners will become her husband) got supplies by wagon train from Magdalena, the round-trip taking about 10 days. There was one phone in town located in the store and a single wire to Magdalena that wind, snow or people taking down poles for firewood often put it out of commission. No electricity except one family with their own small Delco plant for their own house.... Mostly families drew water from dug wells in buckets. There was no church or preacher but we did have Sunday school in the schoolhouse.
>
> As for Prohibition days there were no saloons but no lack of liquor. Saloons and barbershop where man's preserves, women stayed out. No decent woman would ever approach the door of a bar, much less enter.

No movies are entertainment except what we made for ourselves and there was no lack of that. Parties with games, tricks and singing, horseback rides for the young folks and picnics and dances for the old and young, sometimes in impromptu get-togethers and in town, often to the surprise of the hostess, or planned affairs at the "Woodman Hall."Occasionally ranchers would pass the word for all to come to their place for an all-night dance. People came and wagons and on horseback, a few in cars is there was a road to the ranch, some for miles. At midnight and enormous supper was set out and always joking and tricks the boys delighted in playing. Present day "Westerns" bear little resemblance to the way the Cowboys I knew lived and worked. There were, no doubt plenty of rough, thoroughly padded pool Mandarin early days but all the men who survived and were still living in the reserve area in my time or courteous, considerate and kind, even gentle in manner and speech, even those who were reputed to be outlaws or rustlers in their youth.

In those days.... The ranchers drove their cattle the hundred miles or more to the railroad at Magdalena when they sold them in the fall. The drives moved very slowly to allow the cattle to graze along the way and were never hurried or "choused" as it was important to avoid exciting or running the cattle which took off weight more rapidly on the long walk to the railhead where price was figured by weight. The cattle were treated gently but the horses were worked hard, constantly on the move around the perimeter of the herd, keeping them from spreading out to unmanageable size and always on the lookout for strays and unruly animals determined to return the way he had come. This meant that each rider must have no accidents or lost horseshoes for much of the handling a herd depended on the speed and knowledge of the horses.

Horses were not gentle plugs that you could walk behind safely or mount from either side but were high-spirited, sometimes mean and some cowboys would not have horse that lacked the vinegar to do some pitching when first mounted in the morning. Good cow ponies were on their way by the time the writer had his foot in the stirrups to mount.... A good cow pony was often asked to see and respond to situations that called to action by his rider.

The McCarty boys tell the story of one of their drives to the railhead. Uncle Polk had a few head of yearlings to send to the market and asked if he could put them in the McCarty heard for the drive and of course, they were glad to oblige a neighbor but Uncle Polk was a proud man and asked no favor but wanted to do his share of the work. The McCarty's knowing his age, lack of experience or aptitude in horsemanship or the handling of cattle feared he would be a serious hindrance in their work so to avoid offending him refusing his help they asked him to take charge of the remuda or horse herd.

One morning after they had left the mountains, they were out on the plains, Uncle Polk got up as usual, saddled his horse and went out to bring in his charges that were grazing some distance from camp. Before long he brought in the horses but instantly got off his horse head coming to the chuckwagon for breakfast as usual, he turned and rode back the way he had come. They waited a while, keeping food and coffee hot foreign, expecting him to be back soon.... But he did not come. Much puzzled and a little concerned they decided they would have to break camp and get the herd moving expecting him to catch up with them soon.

The morning wore on and finally they saw him coming in. Dude road out to meet him and asked Uncle Polk what was the trouble, what did you go back for? "Well," Uncle Polk drawled, looking down, perhaps a little shamefaced, "I brought them ponies in and I saw Ole Ball wasn't with them so I took out to look for him. I rid and I rid but I couldn't find Ole Ball so I rid and rid some more but still no Ole Ball then.....Ey Gonnine, looked down.... And thar I was aridin him, yes I was."

The new families getting together. Sarah, is taking the photo of Hugh standing, Jean Herrick (mother) sitting with Margaret Fraser (mother) standing next to Marjorie (sister). On the right the string technique is used again to get Sarah in the photo. Taken just before or just after Hugh and Sarah marry.

August 11, 1925. Sarah E. Herrick and Hugh C. Fraser are married in Socorro, New Mexico, and take their Honeymoon in the mountains outside Reserve, New Mexico, camping together.

The string photographic technique is used in this photo of my Grandparents together on their honeymoon.

Looking south down Main Street, Reserve. The Reserve Mercantile is where the two would meet and both worked. Their lives will bloom and expand in Reserve.

Looking down the street and house of the Jack Fraser Family. The Hugh Fraser Family lived three or four houses down the street on the same side.

The Hugh Fraser home in Reserve, New Mexico. 1925–1938.

The Hugh and Sarah Fraser family expands with the birth of Marjorie Ann Fraser, born on January 30, 1928, in Magdalena, New Mexico. My mother Jean Cameron Fraser is born June 28, 1929, in Silver City, New Mexico, not Reserve, for that was the closest doctor at the time. It was a three hour drive to the south. These two photographs were taken in 1930 or 1931 by a traveling professional photographer on their porch and then inside their house in Reserve.

A second photo of the Hugh Fraser Family

Jean Colville Herrick with her three brothers, William, Robert, Charlie. Sister Jessie is not in this photo.

The Jack and Ola Fraser family at their home just up the street from my grandparents home, about 1930 or 1931. Ola is seated at the piano, Helen, Lilian, Johnny, Catherine, Peggy and Jack Fraser with Eleanor, the youngest on his lap.

John Weir, daughter Margaret Jane and son Jack in front of their mother Daisy Fraser Weir, Anna Fraser, Grandmother Margaret Fraser with Marjorie Fraser in front of Sarah Fraser next to her mother Jean Herrick with a young Jean Fraser (Spiller). Hugh Fraser is the last visible person on the right. My mother was three or four years old, 1932 or 1933.

My mother, Jean, is second from the left, in between sisters Evelyn Hext and Barbara Ann Hext. Marjorie Ann is in the dark dress on the right in the Fraser backyard in Reserve. The dog has lost his name over time.

Downtown Reserve looking at the county courthouse from the Mercantile from porch, 1930s.

Road trips that were longer than a day's travel time required sleeping on the ground as layover accommodations. Here is Marjorie and Brad Bradbury, rolling the sleeping roll and mother Herrick is drinking a cup of coffee as the equipment is being put away. This is what it was like to journey from Socorro to Reserve even in the 1930s.

Jean Herrick coming out of the Fitch Building which was the home of the Security Title Abstract Company. It is at the northwest corner of the Socorro plaza. The company was on the second floor for as long and longer than I can remember. My grandfather and I would walk from the office across the plaza to the county courthouse as a general rule when I was little. The Security Title Abstract Company is the only title and abstract company in Socorro and Catron Counties, the two largest, in area, counties in the state of New Mexico and that is a lot of square miles.

Mrs. Margaret Fraser, Hugh's mother, dies June, 20, 1933 in Socorro but is buried in Magdalena in the family plot.

Local color sitting around the Socorro plaza.

My mother on the right and her sister Marjorie are dressed up for a dance recital, Socorro, early 1940s. They are in their "SunBonnet Sue" costumes posing outside the Hilton House where the Family lived when they first moved back from Reserve to Socorro. 1938–1939.

The drug store where my mother worked
in as a young girl in 1942. Downtown Socorro.

This photo shows the drugstore from a corner of the plaza. The electric pole was the development of the town. My mother remembers electricity in Socorro from the mid-1930s.

The Socorro train station and rail head. 1930–1940s.

My dad, Kenneth Dwight Spiller, "Skid," on the right, the only one wearing glasses and sunglasses at that. On the back of the photograph it says "Somewhere on Normandy, June 1944." The stories I remember that I heard growing up were that he was at Omaha Beach for "D-Day" on a "LST" ship in the front of a machine-gun, but his commander told him not to fire the gun for it would draw fire toward them, so the day was spent watching from a distance. He was in the Navy's "Sea Bees" or Construction Battalion and it was said that when the Marines landed there was a sign greeting them as they came on the beach that said "Welcome – the CBs"

This is my mother Jean Fraser, one by herself and the other with her friend Katy Bonnel. They are in front of the University of New Mexico Dorms D & 24, 1947–48. The barracks were moved from Los Alamos, New Mexico, in 1947.

My dad was a gifted musician. He played the violin as a kid, the drums and piano in the Navy and just about anything that was needed to make the band work. The above photo has him playing the piano in the Marty Baum Band while playing a gig at the Casa Manana, March, 1947. He was a student at the University of New Mexico on the GI Bill. Saxes: Dick Baum, Don Sprengeler, George Brown; horns: Joe Pera, Golden Eagan Orlando Wagner (also guitar); bass: Bill Richardson; drums: Llyod Smith and trombone: Marty Baum.

My mother and father marry on August 20, 1949, cutting the wedding cake in Socorro. Both are students at the University of New Mexico.

The four Fraser siblings, Jack, Daisy, Anna and Hugh, 1950s.

Hugh and Sarah on their 50th Wedding anniversary, August 11, 1971.

My grandfather Hugh and my mother Jean, on the train platform at the old Alvarado Hotel and Train Station in Albuquerque, 1950s.

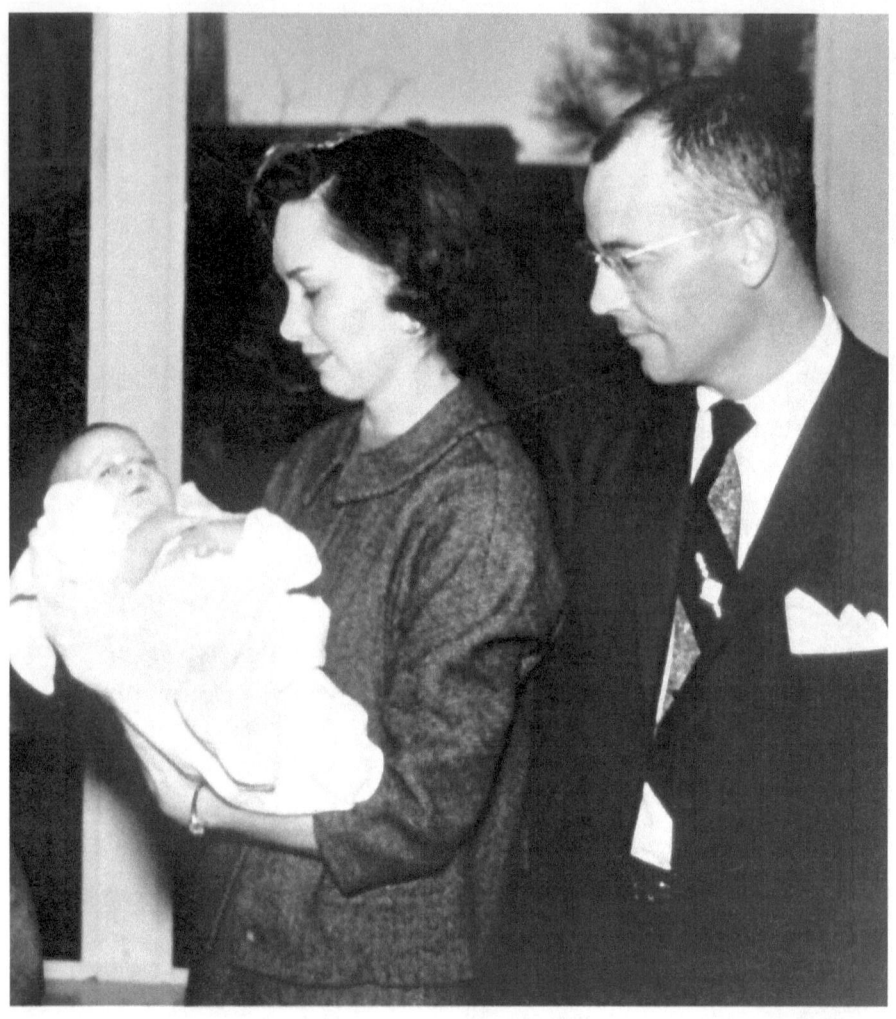

This photo is of me with my parents to start and end this story for now. I was born February 11, 1951, in Albuquerque, New Mexico. I was the first male child born into the New Mexico Herrick/Fraser families in three generations.

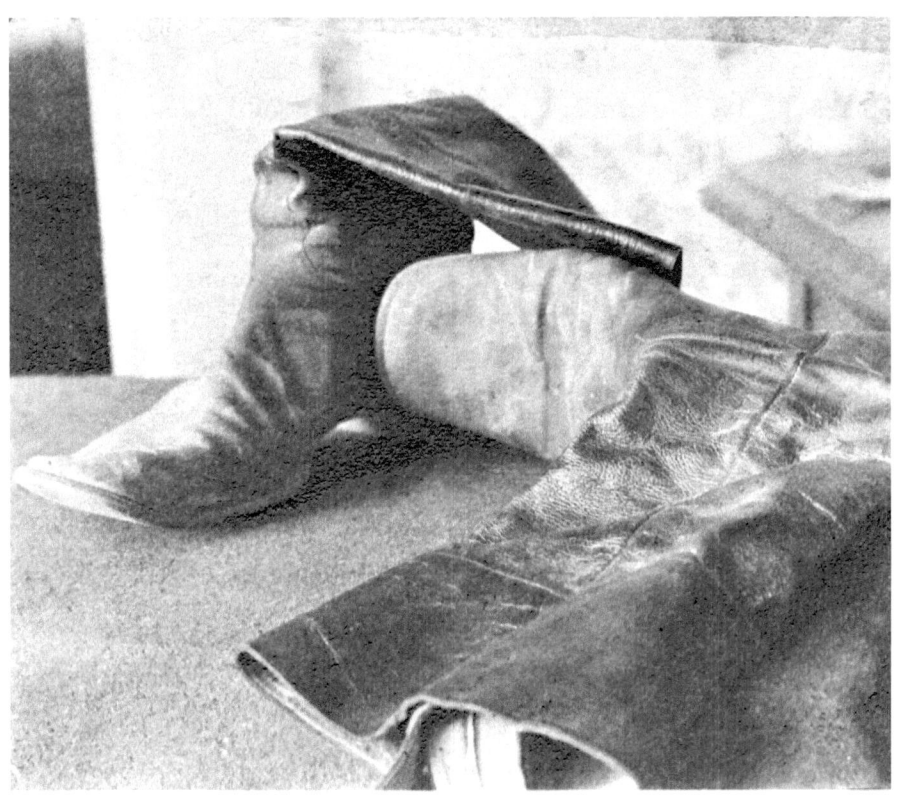

An old pair of empty cowboy boots.

Beulah "Aunt Bunny" Herrick dies November 15, 1971 from injuries from an auto accident in Socorro and Marjorie (Aunt Miggie) Herrick Bradbury, dies December 1, 1972. They are both buried in the family plot in Socorro. My Great Grandmother, Jean Colville Herrick dies at home in Socorro in her sleep.

My grandfather Hugh Cameron Fraser died in 1975 from a stroke in Socorro and is buried in Magdalena, New Mexico and my grandmother Sarah Herrick Fraser dies February 15, 1976 from cancer in Belton, Missouri, where my Aunt Marjorie Fraser Hagan lived but is buried in the family plot in Socorro.

Cancer takes my father, "Skid," Kenneth Dwight Spiller, way too early, October 24, 1990, one month before my second son Jonathan Burton Spiller is born. (November 24, 1990). My older son William Bradford Spiller was born June 24, 1988.

My wonderful mother, Jean Cameron Fraser Spiller, left us on November 4, 2019, after fighting cancer for a few years.

The End for now!

28 January 2022

www.ingramcontent.com/pod-product-compliance
Lightning Source LLC
Chambersburg PA
CBHW020225170426
43201CB00007B/320